# ICELAND ROUNDABOUT

*Books by*
# AGNES ROTHERY

*Biography*
FAMILY ALBUM
A FITTING HABITATION

*Juveniles*
SOUTH AMERICAN ROUNDABOUT
WASHINGTON ROUNDABOUT
CENTRAL AMERICAN ROUNDABOUT
SCANDINAVIAN ROUNDABOUT
MARYLAND AND VIRGINIA ROUNDABOUT
ICELAND ROUNDABOUT

*Essays and Travel*
THE PORTS OF BRITISH COLUMBIA
VIRGINIA, THE NEW DOMINION
NORWAY, CHANGING AND CHANGELESS
DENMARK, KINGDOM OF REASON
FINLAND, THE NEW NATION
SWEDEN, THE LAND AND THE PEOPLE
IMAGES OF EARTH: GUATEMALA
OUR COMMON ROAD
THE HOUSE OF FRIENDSHIP
A GARDEN ROSARY
THE ROMANTIC SHORE
CAPE COD, NEW AND OLD
THE COAST ROAD FROM BOSTON TO PLYMOUTH
NEW ROADS IN OLD VIRGINIA
CENTRAL AMERICA AND THE SPANISH MAIN
SOUTH AMERICA, THE WEST COAST AND THE EAST
ICELAND, NEW WORLD OUTPOST

*Novels*
THE HOUSE BY THE WINDMILL
THE HIGH ALTAR
INTO WHAT PORT?
BALM OF GILEAD

*A Play*
MISS COOLIDGE

# ICELAND ROUNDABOUT

by

## AGNES ROTHERY

ILLUSTRATED BY
GEORGE GRAY

DODD, MEAD & COMPANY
NEW YORK 1948

Copy 1
49/4518

FOR TERRY

WITH LOVE

## ACKNOWLEDGMENT

Grateful acknowledgment is made to Sigrídur Ingimarsdóttir for her clever retelling of the Icelandic tales which appear in this book.

# ICELAND ROUNDABOUT

# CONTENTS

CHAPTER                                                              PAGE

I    WHERE ICELAND IS . . . . . . . . I

II   THE PEOPLE WHO CAME THERE FIRST . . 13

III  REYKJAVIK . . . . . . . . . 21

IV  LIFE IN THE COUNTRY . . . . . . . 31

V   GOING TO SCHOOL . . . . . . . . 42

VI  SOME STRANGE AND WONDERFUL PLACES . . 51

VII  THE OLDEST PARLIAMENT IN THE WORLD . . 63

VIII  RICHES FROM THE SEA . . . . . . . 76

IX  CO-OPS . . . . . . . . . . . 86

X   SOME BIRDS AND ANIMALS IN ICELAND . . 93

XI  OLD WORDS, OLD STORIES AND OLD AND NEW
      BOOKS . . . . . . . . . . 107

XII  SOME ICELANDIC FAIRY TALES, RETOLD BY
      SIGRÍDUR INGIMARSDÓTTIR . . . . . 127

XIII  PIRATES, A PASTOR AND SOME POEMS . . . 144

XIV  A GREAT MAN AND A GREAT BOOK . . . . 155

XV  ICELANDERS AND AMERICANS . . . . . 175

XVI  IN AN ICELANDIC HOME . . . . . . 186

     INDEX . . . . . . . . . . . 197

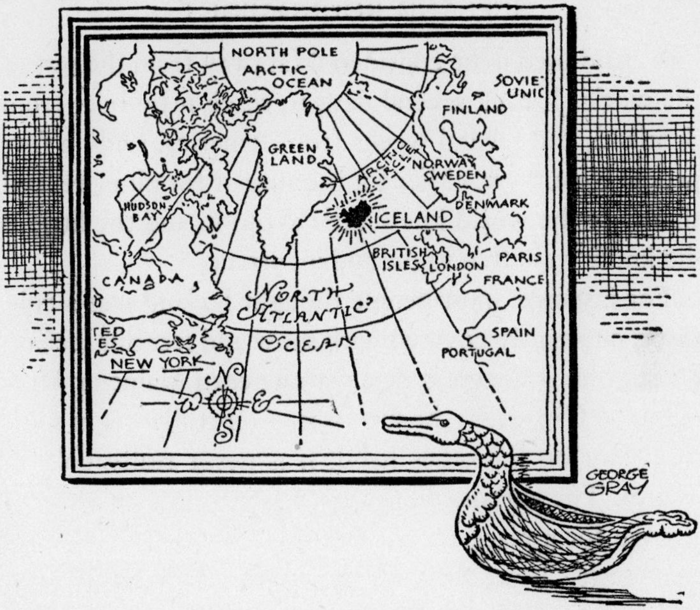
NORTH POLE
ARCTIC OCEAN
FINLAND
GREEN LAND
NORWAY
SWEDEN
DENMARK
HUDSON BAY
ICELAND
BRITISH ISLES
LONDON
PARIS
FRANCE
CANADA
NORTH ATLANTIC OCEAN
SPAIN
PORTUGAL
NEW YORK
GEORGE GRAY

## I. WHERE ICELAND IS

If you will look at your map—and you must look at your map the very first thing—you will see north-west of the British Isles and east of Greenland what looks like a very small island, marked Iceland.

As a matter of fact, it is not so very small compared with other islands in Europe. But it is small compared to our country. It is just about the size of one of our states—Kentucky.

Iceland used to be considered faraway from the rest of the world. It took several days to reach it by boat from Scotland, and several weeks from America. Only a few people went there, either for business or for pleasure, and therefore the world knew little about it, and the little it did know was often vague and incorrect.

For instance, most people thought Iceland was a cold place, constantly covered with snow and ice. But Iceland is not cold: it is a good deal warmer than Maine or Minnesota or Canada. To be sure, it is never really hot in summer—but on the other hand, it is never really cold in winter. The harbors do not even freeze. This may seem strange for a place whose extreme northern tip touches the Arctic Circle, but it is explained by the Gulf Stream, which is a warm, mighty river moving through the cold ocean. A branch of the Gulf Stream encircles Iceland, giving it a year-round temperature about like the year-round temperature of Pennsylvania. If it were not for the Gulf Stream, Iceland would certainly be terribly cold, instead of having weather which is agreeably mild, even in winter.

Today steamers take about ten days to go from the United States to Iceland, but it is possible to take a plane in New York and arrive in Iceland thirteen or fourteen hours later, so it no longer seems faraway. If you write a letter from almost any place in the United States and send it to Iceland by airmail, you may get the answer back in less than a week. On Monday morning the New York Sunday newspapers are for sale in Reykjavik, (pronounced Ray'-ka-vik) which is the capital city. Cablegrams go back and forth between America and Iceland in a few moments and you can telephone over there from here as easily as you can telephone to your next door neighbor at home. People all over Iceland—even in the most faraway and lonely farmhouses—can hear certain important speeches and news from Washington or New York over the radio.

The airplane, the cable, the telephone and the radio have brought Iceland closer to us, and there is no longer any reason why Americans should not know about the wonderful and beautiful things which make this island different from any other place in the world.

It is not only because Iceland is an interesting place and the Icelanders are attractive people that we should know about it, however. It is an extremely important place because of its geographical location. If you will look at your map again, you will see that if a plane from the United States wants to go to England or Denmark or to Norway or Sweden, the shortest route is along a line which runs between Newfoundland and Iceland. This means that planes can stop in Iceland and get gasoline or be repaired. During the Second World War there were more planes coming into and going out of the big airport, which is named Keflavik (pronounced Kef-la-vik) than came and went at La Guardia Field, in New York.

Iceland is sometimes called the steppingstone between North America and Europe, and during the war we had thousands and thousands of soldiers stationed there. We wanted to be sure that no country which was our enemy should get possession of this convenient steppingstone, and be able to use it as a base from which it could easily attack us.

Now that the war is over, we no longer have any soldiers stationed in Iceland. But the huge airport at Keflavik is still there, with its control-tower and mile-long runways, its lights, reflectors, radio, radar, and every known safety device. There is a big terminal building, with a fine restaurant and waiting rooms and a hotel where travelers can spend the night, if they want. The Americans who work there have apartments, if they are married, and if they are single, they have bachelor quarters.

Keflavik is no longer a military airport, but a commercial one. It is no longer an exclusively American airport, but is international, for it is also used by several European and Icelandic airplane companies. It is not even owned by America now, but is under the laws of Iceland. Although most of the men operating it are Americans, and although we paid for all the buildings, Icelanders are being trained to take over these duties. We have made an agreement with Iceland that by 1953, if the Icelanders want, we will give up the field and all the buildings and withdraw our men. Probably Iceland will decide it would rather have us stay, and manage the place, because they have their own busy airport in Reykjavik.

Keflavik today looks very different from the Keflavik our soldiers knew, when all the buildings were Quonset huts. But it is still thirty miles from Reykjavik and it is still a windy, rather disagreeable place, surrounded by bare brown lava fields. Plane passengers who stop off there for an hour on their way to some other country sometimes think that all Iceland must be like Keflavik, and if it is, they are sure it must be a most unattractive country. So the things they tell their friends at home are almost as incorrect as the reports the travelers of long ago brought back.

When you drive from Keflavik to Reykjavik, at first you see practically nothing but bare brown lava fields stretching away in every direction. These were made when volcanoes erupted and the lava poured like rivers down their sides and into the valleys, killing all the trees and grass and leaving only this thick, rough coating, as hard and sharp as rock. When lava finally crumbles, it makes a fertile soil. But it takes a long time for it to disintegrate in this cool climate, so although some of these lava flows are thousands of years old, nothing grows in them but mosses of different colors. The whole country of Iceland is built up on a kind of volcanic substance called basalt, which is piled up in ledges and palisades.

The next thing you will notice on your drive from Keflavik is that there are practically no trees. Perhaps in a sheltered spot around a house there may be two or three little ones and in some places there are what are called forests. We would not call them forests in America, for the trees are small and twisted by the wind, and rarely grow as high as twenty or thirty feet. There is not any wood in the whole of Iceland which can be used for building. All the wood that is used for houses or furniture or tools must be brought from some country across the water, such as England or Sweden or Canada or the United States. Except for driftwood or sometimes a few spindly pieces of birch, there is not even wood for burning.

The interesting thing about this is that, long ago, before men discovered Iceland and came to live on the island, there were many trees—such as walnuts and sequoias, maples, oaks, elms and tulip trees—and they reached a good size. Pieces of trees have been found buried in bogs, and they show just what kind they were and how large they grew.

The first settlers cut all the trees down for building and

for firewood. They had brought sheep with them, and turned them out to graze, and the sheep destroyed all the little new shoots, and made an open meadow or even a bare desert out of what were once woodlands. Today the government is planting lots of trees, such as firs and spruce and larch and other evergreens, and some of these have reached as high as thirty or forty feet. People are planting them around their houses and meadows and on the mountainsides, but there still is no wood which can be used for either building or fuel.

At first you miss trees, but after a while you grow accustomed to the landscape and come to love it, for you can see the shapes and the forms of the mountains and the rolling meadows, of the long, irregular shore line and the rivers and lakes. Nor do you need trees for shade, because whenever there is sunlight, you want all there is of it.

The sunlight in Iceland is different from that in the United States—at least it has different seasons and hours for shining. During the summer, it shines for twenty-four hours and you can read a book at midnight without turning on any light. You don't have to hurry home before dark, because it doesn't get dark. You may see a man out gardening or painting his house at two o'clock in the morning.

In winter, there is sunshine for only a few hours every day, and then the electric lights burn most of the time.

7

There is plenty of electricity, for there are plenty of waterfalls. Even farmhouses faraway from any settlement usually have electricity for lighting and cooking.

There are three ways of getting heat, to make the houses warm and the water hot. First, there is coal, which has to be brought by ships from Europe or America. Second, there is peat. Peat is made from trees or vegetable matter which have changed into a firm, solid substance and is usually found in bogs or marshes, from which it can be dug out. It is then pressed into blocks, and these blocks burn easily. Third, there is natural hot water.

This natural hot water is one of the most remarkable things in Iceland. All over the country, but most frequently in the southern and western parts, are springs where the water comes bubbling out of the ground almost boiling hot. From earliest times, Icelandic women have been able to take their soiled clothes down to the side of a stream where there is such a hot water spring and wash them handily. Many hundreds of years ago a famous man named Snorri Sturlason brought hot water from a spring near his home and led it into a big, circular stone bath he built in the back of his house. Here he would lie and soak while his friends sat around talking and discussing politics and poetry. He even brought the water inside his house, into some of the rooms.

However, the hot water which is used so freely by the

8

Icelanders today is not piped from the springs, but it is drilled for through rock and drawn up to the surface, just as we drill for oil. About twelve miles from Reykjavik there are a great many borings, as the drills are called, and the hot water is pumped up and carried through pipes to a power house. From there it is pumped through a long aqueduct to big towers on a hill outside the city. From the storage tanks it descends through pipes by gravity, down to the houses and shops and hotels in the city. It comes through radiators just as hot water which has been heated by coal or oil comes into our houses. Although it has been brought from so faraway, it is still so hot when you turn on a faucet in the kitchen or bathroom that you have to add cold water to it before you can put your hands in it. All this water is so pure that it can be used for cooking. Another great convenience is that if you have this steaming water in your house, you do not need a furnace, so it does away with the smoke from chimneys and makes the city clean.

The hot water is also used to heat green houses, where people raise potatoes and cucumbers and even melons and bananas, as well as flowers.

It is also piped into many swimming pools, some of which are in handsome tiled buildings and some of which are outdoors. As has been said, in Iceland it is not as cold in winter as it is in many parts of the United States, so the outdoor pools can be enjoyed practically all the year around.

These hot water springs pop up in all sorts of queer places. At Laugar there is a cold brook where there are trout. On top of the cold water there lies boiling hot water from a near-by spring. If you catch a trout and draw it up through the hot water, it is slightly cooked by the time you get it on land. If you want to leave it in the hot water a little longer, it will be thoroughly cooked, all ready to eat. There are other hot springs under the ice of glaciers, and there are still others coming up from the floor of the ocean. To one such place fishermen out in their boats have gone for centuries, when they wanted fresh water, and have drawn it up and used it to quench their thirst, although for miles around there is nothing but salt water, which, of course, cannot be used for drinking.

Besides the hot water springs, there are thousands of others which give cold water. When this is to be piped into the houses, a spring is chosen on the edge of a lava field. The water seeps through the lava, which acts as filter, so it is not necessary to add any chemicals, as we usually have to do in our reservoirs. In fact, the cold water is so absolutely pure that it can be used instead of distilled water in batteries. It is soft and sweet and tastes more delicious than any water in the world, and no one who has ever had a drink of it will ever forget how good it is.

Now you can understand why, although Iceland is so far north, it is not uncomfortably cold. The Gulf Stream keeps the temperature mild, and with all this hot water piped straight into their houses, people can be warm, no matter what the weather is. Although certain vegetables cannot be grown out of doors there, even in summer, many can be raised in greenhouses. The earth around the hot water springs is often warm, so that it is usually easy to raise cabbages outdoors.

In some parts of Iceland there are not enough hot water springs to heat the houses, and coal must be brought in for that purpose. In order that things may be fair for everyone, the government charges those who use the hot water which has been piped in exactly what the other people who are not so lucky have to pay for coal.

It is possible to get electricity almost everywhere, and on the roofs of farmhouses there is often a windmill to give additional power.

In order to build these hot and cold water systems and to provide electricity, the Icelanders had to understand engineering thoroughly, but since they are intelligent and well educated, they mastered these problems quickly.

As you approach Reykjavik, whether you come by

car from the airport at Keflavik or directly to the capital by boat, you will see a city a good deal like an American city, and the first thing you will probably do is to take a walk around it.

But before that you may like to know how Iceland was first discovered and by whom and what it looked like then.

GEORGE
GRAY
ICELAND

## II.    THE PEOPLE WHO CAME THERE
FIRST

WHEN white men first discovered most of the
countries of the world they found that other
men were already living there. There were
Indians in North and South America, Bushmen in Aus-
tralia, Mongolians in Asia, Eskimos in Greenland and
Ethiopians in Africa. All through Europe have been
found buried pieces of chipped stone or pottery, bones,
bits of cloth, and, on the walls inside caves, pictures carved
with sharp stones, proving that human beings had lived
there thousands of years ago.

Iceland is different from these places, because, until
the Vikings came there, a little more than a thousand
years ago, no other race had inhabited the island. Therefore the history of Iceland has no prehistoric period. We

know pretty much what it was like when it was discovered, and we have accurate records of its progress ever since. For this reason, it is considered an extremely young country.

It may not sound young when we read that a Greek, named Pytheas, sailed to it three hundred years before the birth of Christ and wrote a book about it, or that about 800 years after the birth of Christ some Irish monks went there to live so that they would not be distracted by other people. But such dates are recent when we compare them with the ages before then that man has lived on the globe.

The first real discoverers and settlers of Iceland were Vikings. These adventurous men came from Scandinavia and were always sailing around, exploring unknown places. One of them was a man named Floki, who had seen Iceland on one of his voyages and decided he would like to settle there. This was about 860 B. C. He returned to Norway, gathered up some sheep and cows, sailed them over to Iceland, brought them ashore and turned them out to graze. Then he and his companions were so delighted with the plentiful and delicious fish in the surrounding waters that they spent all their time fishing and forgot to cut the grass for hay. As a result, when the winter came, there was no hay for the cattle and they starved to death. The following spring was rather cold. One day Floki went up to the top of a mountain to look out at the fjord, which is a long finger of water extending from the sea between the banks of the land. The fjord he saw was filled with ice. You remember that the harbors and fjords in Iceland never freeze in winter, but sometimes ice floats down from the polar regions and lodges there. This was what Floki saw, and he felt so discouraged, with his cattle dead and the fjord packed with ice, even in springtime, that he decided to leave the place forever and go home. He called the country he had left Iceland, and although that name is not a true description of the island, it has been called so ever since, which is one reason why most people think it must be very cold and covered with ice and snow.

Floki, who was so easily discouraged, is not considered the first settler of Iceland, because he did not stay there long enough to deserve that title.

The first settler was Ingolf Arnason.

Ingolf left Norway because he did not like the way the king was running that country. He had sailed to Iceland and liked it, and decided to return there and make a colony. So in 874 he came back with his brother Leif and with cattle and all sorts of tools for building and farming. Before they left Norway, Ingolf sacrificed to the gods, for this was in pagan times, when such sacrifices were considered necessary. But Leif refused to sacrifice.

When their two boats came in sight of Iceland, Ingolf,

who had brought with him the two wooden pillars of his high seat, or throne, threw them into the ocean, saying that when he found where they had come ashore, on that place he would build his house and lay out his farm.

He didn't find the pillars for a long time—and in the meanwhile he camped in various places and plowed the land. Leif started farming, too, but he made a great mistake. He had only one ox and he needed more than that to pull his plow and break up the soil for planting. Now the Vikings had captured some Irishmen in Ireland and had brought them along as slaves. Leif made some of these captives pull his plow and this quite naturally made the Irishmen angry. They had never been slaves before, but freemen, and had no intention of being treated in this fashion. They promptly killed Leif and ran away. Ingolf found them later and killed them in punishment, but that didn't do Leif any good. Ingolf and his friends, who were all pagans, were sure this was because Leif had refused to sacrifice to the gods.

It was nearly three years before Ingolf found his pillars. Just as had said he would do, he took a large tract of land where they had drifted ashore and started his farm. This is the place where Reykjavik now stands, and the first thing you see when you arrive there is a low hill, on top of which is a great bronze statue of Ingolf.

Other Norwegians came to join Ingolf and gradually

the settlement grew. By and by they called themselves Icelanders, instead of Norwegians, but their language and customs were similar to those of Norway.

Since there were no savages to civilize or subdue, but only the Norsemen and a few Irish, the settlers did not have to waste any time in fighting or defending themselves. They could get right to work founding a republic.

This republic was the very first to be established north of the Alps, and it was organized so well that, although it had ups and downs, it still exists. Its Parliament—called the Althing—is centuries older than the British representative body, so that Iceland is sometimes called the Mother of Parliaments.

It would not be correct to think that everything went smoothly from that day to this, and that the Iceland we see now merely grew without any setbacks into the present excellently-run modern country.

Although the Icelanders eventually accepted Christianity as the national religion, and although they organized such a good Parliament, they did not have any central authority to enforce their laws, and soon all the small chieftains began quarreling among themselves. They quarreled so long and so fiercely that finally they decided to ask Norway, which was, after all, their mother country, to help them keep the peace. And in that way Norway gained control over the island. Later Denmark gained that control, and for many centuries the Icelanders were not really free, as they had hoped to be, but were a colony and had to obey Danish laws.

At one time Denmark even made them give up the Althing.

Besides being dominated first by Norway and then by Denmark, terrible calamities befell the country.

There are hundred and hundreds of volcanoes in Iceland. In fact, it is the most volcanic country in the world. When a volcano erupts there, it may be preceded by earthquakes, and then smoke and fire soar up into the sky and lava pours forth and ruins the farming land. Ashes may be borne by the wind as faraway as Scotland: poisonous gases kill men and women and children and animals.

For about four hundred years volcanoes kept erupting in Iceland—some of them so violently that they killed a third of the population. After such an eruption, there would be a famine, for the grass would be destroyed and the animals had nothing to eat. And after the famine there would be disease, which would kill more people. So these were dreadful centuries for Iceland. Everyone was fearfully poor, and furthermore, the inhabitants were all unhappy because of the power Denmark held over their country.

Iceland has never had an army or a navy or gone to war with any other country. But this does not mean they es-

caped bloodshed, for various bands of pirates came
ashore and set fire to the houses and stole what they could,
and even carried some of the Icelanders off as slaves.

So altogether Iceland had a hard time of it.

Most of the old travel books, which were written by
Englishmen and Americans, describe how miserable life
in Iceland was. Houses were low, dark hovels, made of
dirt and stone; the roads were merely muddy paths, and
there was poverty and sickness and sadness everywhere.

Today all these things have changed. Iceland is no
longer a colony of Denmark, but is once again an independent and progressive republic, with a President, an
Althing with an upper and a lower chamber like our Congress, with its own laws, money and flag. It is no longer
poor, but very prosperous. In fact, there is nowhere any
poverty such as exists in the slums of our cities. People are
no longer sickly and half-starved, but are well fed and
one of the healthiest races in the world. They are no
longer sad, but full of life and good spirits and friendly to
strangers.

Even the volcanoes seem to be behaving pretty well.
To be sure, occasionally one acts up. In March, 1947,
Hekla, which is the biggest, erupted, after having been
quiet for more than a hundred years. But although it was
a tremendous eruption and the smoke and fire lingered in
and over the crater for months, the lava did not destroy

any villages or farms.

Iceland today is not at all like the poor country described by travelers fifty years ago. If you read this book, you will see what it is really like now and why the Icelanders love it, and why many visitors love it, too, and hope to visit it again and again.

III.                                          REYKJAVIK

IF you come to Reykjavik by boat, you will enter the
big harbor, with great piers and docks and all kinds
of modern loading machinery. There are light-
houses to guide the sailor at night, and there are tall buildings—such as the Navigation School and the Roman
Catholic Cathedral—on the hilltops.

Around the harbor are office buildings and store houses
made of concrete, just like similar buildings in the United

States. The streets that lead into the city are paved, with sidewalks, and shops and hotels line them. Some of the shops are only one story high, but there are other buildings of five and six stories, with elevators. There are hotels and restaurants and government buildings, and a number of open parks, with statues and benches and green grass and, in summer, beds of bright flowers. Flowers grow well because the summers are cool, the sunlight lasts for many hours and there are frequent showers. In fact, the grass and flowers are so fine, you hardly miss shade trees.

There are moving picture houses, a big modern theatre, schools, churches, single houses, double houses and apartment houses.

The buses come from all directions into the central square. There are taxis and automobiles—private automobiles, many of them imported from America—trucks, jeeps and bicycles, so that at certain hours the uniformed policemen are busy directing traffic.

The Icelandic boys and girls on the streets are blonde or brunette, with an occasional redhead. They are dressed just like the boys and girls in your home town. The women and older girls have their hair waved in beauty shops and their fingernails manicured and use face powder and lipstick, just as they do in the United States. If you met these people in New York, you would

think they were New Yorkers. Nearly all of them speak English and if you ask them a question, they will answer you promptly and correctly and probably go out of their way to show you a direction.

Some of the older women prefer to wear the traditional Icelandic costume. This consists of a long, full skirt, with a bodice laced with gold or silver cord over a blouse. The hat is a kind of flat tam o'shanter with a long tassel and it is most becoming. The women also wear an apron,

23

which is really a decorative part of the costume, for it may be of heavy silk, like the blouse, or of some other pretty material. If they need a wrap, they wear a shawl or long coat. The young people do not wear this national costume often, only when they dress up for some festival or celebration, but a good many of them keep the embroidered wedding dresses of their mothers and grandmothers for such occasions. When there is a wedding or christening or some other big affair, the women often wear a high white headdress with a veil.

But most of the people on the street are dressed just as Americans are: the girls often without hats, and in bobby sox. When they go hiking or picnicking, they wear slacks and sweaters. The very little children are usually in pretty knitted suits and caps, which their mothers have made and embroidered.

As you walk around Reykjavik, one of the first things you will notice is the number of bookstores. There are fifty thousand people in Reykjavik, and if you compare that number with the population of some American towns you know, you will get an idea of its size. There are between thirty and forty bookstores of good size and they are all busy. In them are books not only in Icelandic and in other foreign languages, but in English as well. You can find almost any good classic—such as Dickens and Hawthorne and Thackeray and Shakespeare, and almost any popular American best seller, such as *Gone with the Wind,* or *The Egg and I.* There are lots of books for younger readers such as *Little Women* and *Pollyanna.* Some of these are translated and others are in English, for nearly all Icelanders read English and understand it. American magazines and newspapers are on the counters. At the movies are the same films Americans see at home and the audiences are able to follow all the conversations and jokes.

The next thing you may notice is the number of florists' shops, for although there are so many flowers in beds, in the parks and in people's yards, and although there are wild flowers everywhere, the greenhouses are growing more and more things every day and can always be sure of selling them,—roses, pinks, sweat peas, gladioli and all sorts of potted plants filled with blossoms. There are plenty of flowers in Iceland all summer long, and when winter comes, there are still flowers. In nearly every window you will see plants in pots, and in some houses, there are charming conservatories, opening directly out of the living room or dining room. It takes a lot of time to take care of even a small conservatory, but Icelanders love flowers so much, they do not mind the work of tending them.

There are other shops in Reykjavik which seem almost precisely like those in any American town. The canned vegetables and fruits and cereals have familiar trade marks, and so do the soaps and washing powders and toilet articles. Before the war, Iceland used to buy these things from England, but during the war, England was unable to furnish and ship as much as she had been doing, so Iceland began to buy from the United States. Not only most of her automobiles, but also her typewriters and telephones and radios, kitchen utensils and farm machinery are American made.

Some of the shops are different from ours, however. For instance in a drugstore, nothing is sold but drugs and medicines and doctors' supplies. If you want a soda or a milk shake, you go to another shop, where only soft drinks are sold and served in glasses or in paper cups, with straws which came from America. If you want milk, you do not go to the grocery store, but to white-tiled shops where nothing is sold except milk and cream and butter and a sort of cottage cheese called skyr, which is delicious. There are little shops which sell only coffee and cakes, and others which sell only phonograph records. The few big department stores are really only a number of small specialized shops under one roof.

One reason why so many things are imported and have American or English names is that Iceland manufactures only a few articles. You read in Chapter I that the country has no wood which can be used for furniture or building.

Every piece of timber and lumber, everything made of
wood from telegraph poles to broom handles, must be
bought abroad. Neither is there any metal in Iceland.
Every bit of iron or copper or brass or silver, every pot
and pan and pail and key and nail and screw must be
brought in. The glass in the windows, the bottles in the
shops, every piece of paper, the sheets and pillowcases
on the beds, all come from some other country. Although
there are some shops where furniture is made, they have
to buy the raw materials abroad. Only recently has some
pottery been fashioned from different native clays.

The Icelanders cannot raise cotton or flax, so all the
cotton cloth and linen are imported. The only materials
which they raise at home are wool and hides, so they can
make blankets and woolen curtains and rugs, and they can
manufacture shoes and handbags.

The Icelanders are so used to foreign things that they
don't think about them as foreign. But if you should sit
in an Icelandic room and look at every article in it, you
would have quite a lesson in geography. The furniture
may have come from Denmark, Norway or England
and look very modern. The curtains may be of French
voile. The coffee—for you will be offered a cup of coffee
wherever you go at any hour—came from Brazil. The
sugar came from Cuba, the cigarettes from Virginia and
the matches from Sweden, the dainty tablecloth from

Madeira or Ireland. The flour for the delicious little cakes which are served with the coffee undoubtedly came from the United States or Canada. If you spend the night in a private home, you will probably find a tiled bathroom with familiar fixtures, and a neat kitchen with an electric or gas stove, and in many cases an electric refrigerator. But when you go to bed, you will have a surprise. There are no sheets: a big, soft, warm down puff is buttoned or tied into a clean white case, and you roll up in that. You will be warm enough, but it may take a little time to learn to sleep without sheets or blankets. In the morning these down puffs are taken off the beds, and put away in a chest. Then a blanket or a coverlet of some kind is spread over the bed, which is now used as a sofa.

Reykjavik is built on hills, with the water making a long, irregular shore line around it and with splendid mountains behind it. Some of these are pointed and some are rounded and some are flat topped. When the sunlight shines on them, they take on all sorts of rich and delicate tints, and the colors are always changing.

Since there is so little smoke in the air, it is very clear and one can see great distances, so it is hard to realize that a mountain which looks quite near may really be many miles away.

The oldest houses in Reykjavik are only one or two stories high and are built of wood or stucco or even perhaps faced with corrugated tin, but there is now a law that all new buildings inside the city limits must be made of reinforced concrete. Because of possible earthquakes, they are built in the most substantial manner imaginable— with the inside walls and floors of concrete, as well as the outside walls. This concrete is of different shades—some is almost white and some is almost black, and the roofs may be flat or pointed and made of slate or tile or tin. The buildings look rather bare, for, although it is possible to have trees in such places as are protected from the wind, most people have not yet planted any evergreens along the foundations. Once in a while there is a house with vines, but there are not many of these and they die down in autumn. Then the only green is the row of potted plants on the window sills, but it is a poor house indeed which does not have flowerpots and vines in its windows.

Life in Reykjavik is like life in any city. The men go to their offices or to work at the docks or on the roads. The women keep house and go to church and to concerts and to the movies. They go marketing and have their clubs and take care of their children. The boys and girls go to school and after they have graduated, many of the girls have jobs as stenographers and private secretaries and clerks and waitresses. The boys play football after school and go skiing on holidays in winter.

But when we travel we usually like to see things that are different from those that we are accustomed to at home. All of us are used to automobiles, telephones, radios and bathtubs, so it is no novelty to see these same things in Reykjavik.

If we want to see the things that make Iceland different, we must leave the city and go out into the country, and visit the farms and the wilder regions. Then we will begin to understand more truly what Iceland and Icelanders are like.

GEORGE
GRAY
ICELAND

## IV.               LIFE IN THE COUNTRY

THERE are very few people in Iceland compared with its size—only 130,000. About one-third of this number live in the country and make their living by farming.

If you leave Reykjavik to travel around Iceland, you may go on a coastal steamer, which will be clean and comfortable. It will take several days to sail completely around the island, but you will see only the ports where the boat stops. If you take an airplane, you can fly from one end of the island to the other in two hours, but you will not see the people and places as closely as if you were driving.

So the best way to see the country is by bus or automobile, for this way you will see the mountains and deserts and waterfalls, the meadows and farms, the houses and animals and the villages, the towns and the schools.

You can't go by train, for there are no railroads. The country is so mountainous it would be very expensive to build a railroad and keep it in repair. People who are born in Iceland and have never been away from there have never seen a steam engine or a train of cars, except in the movies. However, they get around very satisfactorily by bus and boat and plane and never miss trains or trolleys.

The road around Iceland is quite new. Until 1930, the only way to go by land from Reykjavik, which is in the south and the largest city, to Akureyri, which is in the north and the second largest city, was by foot or pony back. As the distance is 285 miles, it took a long time to make the trip, so most travelers went by boat. The mail for places which were not where boats stopped along the coast was carried on by a man on a pony or on foot only fifteen times a year.

Even now, the road does not go completely around

the country, for in the southeast there is a huge glacier—the largest in Europe—which flows into the sea, so that it is impossible to build a road there. That part of Iceland can still be reached only by boat, on foot or with a pony.

There is just one road for the bus to take and it winds and twists along the coast, goes through mountain passes, skirts bogs and marshes, and leads over deserts and rocky plateaux. It is not wide enough for cars to pass unless one of them draws up to the side in one of the little places which have been constructed for this purpose. It is not a paved road, but made of gravel and stones and in places it is so rough that the bus pitches around and everybody gets bumped and jostled. Although there are bridges over the biggest rivers, there are lots of little streams which have no bridges and then the bus goes splashing through the water.

Nobody minds the bouncing around. In fact, the passengers enjoy the ride so much that usually they all join together and sing most of the way. Every few hours the bus stops at an inn and everyone piles out and gets coffee and cakes, so altogether the trip is great fun.

It takes thirteen or fourteen hours for the trip between Reykjavik and Akureyri and if it weren't for stopping for coffee and a good stretch, it would be a pretty tiresome journey.

If you will look at your map again, you will see that

three-fourths of Iceland is desert, or glaciers or lava. This means that the only places people can live are fertile strips along the coast, or in the valleys or beside the fjords. However, there is plenty of room for them there. Each farm is widely separated from its neighbors, for it is necessary to have enough space for the sheep and cows to graze.

If you have seen big farms in the United States, you may not think these in Iceland are farms at all, for, although there may be a good sized house and barn and outbuildings, there are no fields of grain or corn or vegetables, except potatoes. There is only grass.

This grass is rich and makes good food for the animals, and when it is cut and dried it provides enough hay to keep them through the winter. A farmer can get two crops of hay in during the summer and sometimes three crops. As it rains a good deal in Iceland, it is quite a problem to get the hay dried. Nowadays, some of the farmers have wind drying machines in their barns, and these are a great help, for they can dry the hay in a few days. If the air that is blown through the machine is heated, it will dry the hay in a few hours.

A farmer with twenty-five acres of cultivated land, a patch of potatoes, a hundred and fifty sheep, five cows and ten ponies can make a good living. Besides the cultivated land around the house, he has grazing land back in the mountain valleys where the sheep and cows stay all summer.

Because most of the animals are grazing faraway, you may not realize how many sheep there are in Iceland as you motor along the road. You will see mother sheep and their lambs and some big rams, but these are only the few stay-at-homes of the half a million in the country. These sheep give wool for clothing and blankets and rugs. Their hides are made into leather, and their flesh is the principal meat the Icelanders have. Twice a year, the sheep are rounded up, all of them to be sheared and some of them to be slaughtered.

The farmers go out on pony back with their herd dogs, down into the valleys and up on the mountains. It may take them several days to find the sheep and drive them to a central place, where there is a big pen, opening into smaller pens. All of the sheep are first driven into the large section, and then each farmer picks out his own and drives them into a smaller pen. He can recognize them by the marks he has put on their ears. This roundup, as it is called, is a sort of neighborhood celebration, when the farm people look forward to seeing their friends and exchanging news.

Usually the sheep are kept sheltered on the farm during the winter, but in places where the weather is mild, they are left out the year round. They are rather small sheep and their wool is coarse, but they are the kind the Icelanders prefer because they don't eat much.

The cows are kept for their milk, and when they are too old to give any more, they are used for food. But there aren't any great, big, fat steers to get beefsteaks from, and the beef isn't very juicy and tender. But the milk and butter and cream are excellent, and that is why the cows are valuable in Iceland.

In some places there are a few goats, and these, too, give milk from which a sweet brown cheese is made.

In one place in the north there are reindeer, the ancestors of which were brought over from Norway more than a hundred years ago, and these, too, can be used for food at certain seasons.

It is always fun to see animals eating and sleeping and frolicking in the fields, but the animals in Iceland which are the prettiest and the most playful and the greatest pleasure to watch are the ponies which the people there call Icelandic horses. They are not as small as Shetland ponies, but a good deal smaller than our horses. They are stocky and strong, with gentle faces and flowing manes and tails. Some are brown and some are black and some are black and white, like circus horses. But whatever their color, they have a grand time when they are out at pasture. They romp and race and kick up their heels and they nibble at one another like kittens.

When a car goes by, they look up in the friendliest way and then toss their heads and gallop off. They are extraordinarily keen-sighted and sure-footed, and can carry a big man easily through streams and over marshy or hummocky fields. They swim across wide rivers with swift currents, and when they scramble out, they do not slip on the smooth, wet banks or stumble on a beach with loose rocks.

The Icelandic farmer could not make a living without his ponies. They not only carry him, but they pull his cart to market, piled high with milk cans or fleeces. At haying time, they carry such big loads of hay that all you can see of these willing helpers is their heads and feet. A row of ponies with these large bundles of hay tied on each side looks like a procession of some queer animals you have never seen before. For centuries the only way of getting anywhere in Iceland besides walking was on pony back. Now that there are roads and automobiles and trucks,

37

a farmer does not need as many of these useful, obedient little creatures as he once did, but he must keep quite a few to help him with his farming. In the towns, as well as in the country, there are ponies, used for riding. Even very little children in Iceland can ride well.

Of course, there is a dog or two on every farm, and some chickens and sometimes a pig. But pigs eat so much that there are not a great many of them, so there is not much ham or bacon or pork.

Now all these animals, except the cats, dogs and chickens, live on grass, although some of the farmers buy grain abroad in addition. So you can see what a calamity it is when a volcano erupts and covers the grassland with lava. The government is now experimenting with raising grain and thinks that before long grain will be grown in many places throughout the country.

There are not many wild animals in Iceland. There are no bears, lions or tigers, and there is not a single snake. There are a few wild foxes—and sometimes, in spite of the dogs, they kill a few sheep. There are other foxes which are kept in pens and raised for their fur. There are some mink, too, raised for the same purpose. Since there is not a zoo in the whole country, Icelandic children have never seen an elephant or a rhinoceros or any similar animal, except in pictures or in the movies.

In the old days, Icelandic farmhouses were hardly more than huts. Since wood was so scarce and costly, the farmer could afford only a few timbers for his roof and perhaps a few boards. He made a small, one-story house of earth and stones, packed sod around it and covered the roof with sod, too. The grass grew green on the roofs and the little dwellings seemed part of the fields in which they stood. Sometimes the animals were kept on the first floor during the winter, and the family lived upstairs in the attic. When they didn't have any glass for the windows, they stretched a piece of sheep's membrane across the opening. They cooked on a peat fire, in an open fireplace, and all of them ate and slept and worked in the one room.

There are still some of these turf huts left in the country, and sometimes they are used to shelter animals or store potatoes. But they never lasted very long and now when they fall down, they are not rebuilt in the old-fashioned way.

Nowadays a farmhouse may be made of wood or concrete and is entirely comfortable. It is well heated with coal or natural hot water, or in some faraway places, with peat. There are so many waterfalls in Iceland that it is usually possible for farmhouses to have electricity. The farm families use it for cooking and for their electric refrigerators, most of which are imported from the United States. Many of them have a radio.

On the east coast there are larger vegetable and finer flower gardens and more trees than in the south or north or west.

There is plenty to eat on an Icelandic farm, although there may not be a great deal of variety. There is mutton from the farmer's own sheep, and potatoes and perhaps a few carrots from his own garden. Fresh salmon and trout come from a near-by river or lake and salt codfish is brought inland from the shore. The cows give milk, and the mother and the daughters make butter and skyr, which you may remember is something like cottage cheese.

Rhubarb grows wild everywhere—in a back yard, in

an open field, even on the top of a grass-roofed hut. People gather it in big baskets and bring it home and make it into pies and puddings and sauces. What is left over they make into jam or preserves. Currants grow well, too, and currant bushes make an edge for many lawns in the cities. When a strong wind whips them, the sidewalk may be quite red with the bright berries. There are other kinds of berries, including blueberries, which are eaten fresh and also made into jam and jelly.

Practically the only things that have to be bought at the store by the farm people are flour, coffee, sugar and salt.

Every Icelandic boy knows how to work on a farm, and every Icelandic girl knows how to cook and clean and sew and knit. In the evenings there is time to read and to tell stories and listen to the radio. When the boys grow older, some of them travel to Canada or to the United States to study newer and better ways of farming. Before the war, they frequently went to England or to the continent to learn about these things.

Of course, in the winter the girls and boys all go to school, and these schools are so splendid that you will be interested to read about them in the next chapter.

CHILDREN in Iceland are wonderfully healthy. Fewer little babies die there than in any country in Europe. Parents are kind and gentle with their sons and daughters and treat them almost as if they were grown-ups. They have great freedom, are happy and cheerful and rarely have to be punished.

And every single one of them, no matter where he or she lives, must go to school.

In the cities and towns there are schools from the primary grades through grammar and high school, and at Reykjavik there is a big university to which any Icelandic boy or girl may go without paying anything. But all the children in faraway places cannot go to Reykjavik, so there are district schools which they can reach by bus. Where the distances are too great for children to travel back and forth every day, they are sent to boarding schools.

Many of these boarding schools are big, modern buildings and whenever it is possible, they are built near hot springs so the pupils can have their own swimming pools. About seventy-five or a hundred boys and girls can be taken care of in such a school at one time. Sometimes the students are divided into troops, each troop attending for twelve or thirteen weeks a year.

In some places there are what are called movable schools because their teachers move from one school to another at different seasons. All of these schools are supported by the state and are free, but there are also some private schools.

In any case, no child is permitted to grow up in Iceland without being thoroughly educated. Of course, the students learn reading and writing, arithmetic, geography and history, but they have to learn a great many other things too. The boys are taught sloyd, or manual training,

because the Icelanders have, from very earliest times, been fond of carving and good carpentry. The girls are taught needlework, because this is an accomplishment every Icelandic woman must master. In many an Icelandic home you may see a chest or a table which the father or one of his sons has carved and decorated in his leisure hours, and on the walls will hang pieces of needlework which have been done by the mother or her daughters. Sometimes this needlework is a picture of a mountain or a waterfall embroidered in silk. Sometimes it is a square of woolen cloth, woven in a decorative pattern. The girls learn how to take the wool from the sheep, card it—which means combing and cleaning it with a wire brush—and spin it into thread. Sometimes they use this in its natural color—

which may be white or black or brown. Sometimes they make dyes from native plants.

Besides sloyd for the boys and needlework for the girls, both boys and girls must study drawing and singing. Icelanders are extremely fond of singing and a great number of them have splendid voices. After they have left school, many of them join choral societies in the towns and villages where they live and meet to practice and to give concerts.

You might think that all these subjects were quite enough to keep boys and girls busy at school. But there is another subject which is very important indeed. This is languages. Since almost no one speaks Icelandic except the Icelanders themselves, it is necessary for the natives to master other languages, if they want to talk to people from other countries or to read books in other tongues. There are ten towns in Iceland and each of them has a grammar school which prepares for the University. In these grammar schools the pupils must study English and Danish from two to four years, and in the four upper classes they must study German and French and Latin. They must do more than study these five languages. They must learn to speak them, understand them and read them. If you have ever studied even one foreign language, you have found that it is not enough to know a few words. If it is to do you any good, you must be able to

45

say what you want in that language and to understand what is answered. In Iceland, children learn foreign languages so thoroughly that they can use them properly. When they go to the movies, they can understand what the actors and actresses are saying, whether they are speaking in English, French, German or Danish.

Besides these regular elementary schools and grammar schools, there are all sorts of special schools, such as agricultural schools for the boys and domestic schools for the girls. There are normal schools to train teachers, and there is a big navigation school in Reykjavik where boys learn all about ships and the sea.

The University at Reykjavik is just like one of our big state universities, except that a few professional courses are not given there. If students want a degree in these subjects, they usually go abroad for a few years.

Now although all these schools are supported entirely or in part by the Government and are free, it is often necessary for students to earn money during their vacations, to pay for their room and board, so it is quite usual for masculine University students to work on farms or on boats, during the summer, and for girls to work, too, at various tasks in offices, hotels, restaurants and other people's homes. For this reason, almost everyone in Iceland is familiar with life outside his or her own particular orbit and comes to realize how important farming, catering, merchandising, fishing and the various other industries are.

Schooling in Iceland means more than studying books. No child can graduate from grade school without learning to swim. If there is no swimming pool at the school to which he goes in winter, during the summer he must go to one where there is such a pool.

There are schools which train teachers of gymnastics, for the Icelanders are fine athletes. One of the most popular games which most Icelandic boys know is called Glima. This is a form of wrestling, and has been practiced in Iceland for more than a thousand years. Two opponents, each wearing a girdle around his waist and another around his thighs, stand facing one another. Each grasps the other by taking hold of the waist girdle with the right hand and taking hold of the thigh girdle with the left hand. The two contestants then move to the left, standing erect, and try to toss or throw each other by lifting or twisting. They must never look down at their feet, but keep their eyes fixed over each other's shoulders, since the rule of the game is that the wrestling must be by touch and feeling and not by sight. The name "Glima" means quickness or something that happens very suddenly and our English word "glimpse" comes from it. Icelandic wrestlers took part in the Olympic games in Stockholm and Berlin. In 1936, Iceland won a European championship in track and field.

In a city like Reykjavik, there are playgrounds for very little children. Some of these which are in the closely built up parts of the city are set behind low walls, and you have to pass through a turnstile or gate to get into them. Here, in a big, clean, safe enclosure, with grass and flower beds around the edges, are swings and slides, sandboxes and seesaws. Little boys and girls wheel or carry or lead their littler brothers and sisters to such places and keep an eye on them while they themselves roll hoops or race their tricycles. There is always an older person to watch over the playground, and see that nobody gets hurt or lost. Of course, these playgrounds are free, so every child—even if he lives in an apartment and has not a yard of his own to play in—has a place to romp, while the mothers are glad to know that some older person is there to take care of any bump or bruise and settle any quarrel.

There are Boy and Girl Scouts in Iceland, just as there are in the United States. They wear a similar uniform and learn the same things as American scouts. They like to hike and camp and ski, and there are many mountain huts where ski runners may stay over night.

As for other sports—such as football, hand batball, golf, tennis, badminton, boxing, rowing, etc.,—there is plenty of space for these, for Iceland is not crowded—not even in the cities. Besides having space, the Icelanders also have time, for in summer when the sunlight lasts so long, football games or tennis matches may be held after supper.

With all these sports and with all the outdoor work on the farms and on the sea, it is no wonder that Icelanders are strong and sturdy and independent. At the same time, such a thing as a child growing up and not knowing how to read and write is unknown. Every single person in Iceland is educated and speaks in the same educated way. A child that is born and brought up in a city uses the same tone of voice and pronounces words in the same way as a child who has been born and brought up on an isolated farm and may never have been to any city or even to a town.

These healthy boys and girls develop into healthy men

and women and, although there are hospitals and doctors, there is less sickness here than in most countries.

For these sturdy Icelanders, one of the most popular ways to spend a holiday is to take long hikes. Sometimes they go by bus part of the way and then get out and explore, for there are many strange and beautiful sights to see and they never tire of visiting them. Some of these will be described in the next chapter.

Mt. HEKLA

GEORGE
GRAY
ICELAND

VI.                    SOME STRANGE AND
                       WONDERFUL PLACES

Yᴏᴜ have been told that there are a great many
      volcanoes in Iceland—and if you go there you
      will see them almost anywhere you look. You
might not know they were volcanoes unless it were
pointed out to you, but think they were mountains or
hills, some of them with pointed tops and some with
flat tops. But a volcano is different from an ordinary
mountain or hill, because it has a deep, bowl-shaped hole,

51

or crater in it, through which fire and lava and smoke or gas and sometimes mud and water push up when the volcano erupts.

In extremely old volcanoes, this crater may have cooled gradually and become filled with earth or covered with snow, so people think it will never be active again and call it extinct. But volcanoes which have been considered extinct sometimes erupt suddenly, to everyone's surprise.

This is what happened with Hekla, in March, 1947.

Hekla is the largest of all the volcanoes in Iceland and in the old days it often did a great deal of damage. Then it was perfectly quiet for a hundred and twenty-two years. The Icelanders have always thought that Hekla was beautiful because of its shape and color and great height —about five thousand feet. Before the days of automobiles, people used to ride out to Hekla from Reykjavik on pony back. They would take several days, camping on the way, and then climb up the steep side of the quiet volcano and peer down into the crater.

Then in March, 1947, Hekla went off with a terrific explosion. The smoke which shot up from the crater was higher than the smoke from the Bikini bomb. Fire blazed and lava poured down the sides and covered about ten square miles. Fortunately, there were no villages or farms where the lava flowed, so no one was killed. The smoke and fire hung above the crater for months, and as soon as it was safe, people came from all over the country to look at the burning mountain. They came in private automobiles and in buses, and some of them flew over the crater in planes. If the night was dark, they could look right down and see the crater glowing red.

The lava stayed hot for a long, long time, so that if you put a piece of paper on it, the paper was scorched. Even after the lava cooled, and Hekla went to sleep again, people kept coming to see it. Every Saturday during the summer, buses are crowded with boys and girls and men and women, in tramping clothes and stout shoes, going out to climb up Hekla. It takes almost a day to drive to its base, and, except for the paved streets in a few cities, most of the roads in Iceland are rather rough, as has been pointed out. When the busload gets to the foot of Hekla, some of the passengers spend the night in a near-by farmhouse, while others creep into the sleeping bags they have brought with them. The next day they all climb up as near the crater as they dare and then climb down again, and then pile into the bus for the long drive back to Reykjavik, singing happily as they bump ahead.

There are other volcanoes which have done even more damage than Hekla. Some of these, in the western part of the country, are under glaciers—which are rivers of ice, fed by snow which remains the year around on the mountaintops. The glaciers move so slowly down the slopes, they seem to be still. But their progress can be measured, even if it can't be seen. When a volcano which is under a glacier erupts, the snow and ice, as well as fire and lava, are hurled into the sky. Sometimes there is so much water that it floods many miles, and human beings and animals are drowned. Ashes and poisonous gases float great distances and the lava destroys the fields.

Between 1300 and 1800 there were so many earthquakes and volcanic eruptions that nine thousand people died, since the cows and sheep on which they depended for food had nothing to eat and starved to death. Besides these calamities, a frightful disease called the Black Death killed two-thirds of the population and after that smallpox killed a third of those left. It was no wonder that the foreigners who visited the country during those years and told or wrote about it, said that the Icelanders were a sad and poverty-stricken people.

There have not been such disastrous eruptions for many years or any plagues like the Black Death, and Icelanders are now cheerful and well off. They have plenty of good grazing land for their cows and sheep and they no longer think of misfortune when they see a lava field. As a matter of fact, artists consider these tumbled, brown stretches, which are often covered with softly colored mosses and lichens, fascinating to paint. Holiday makers especially enjoy traveling to Lake Myvatn, to admire the strange lava forms there.

This lake, which is in the northern part of Iceland, is about twenty miles long, but quite shallow. Hot water flows into it in some places and ice cold water in others. The surface is dotted with small islands, most of which were once active volcanoes, and more of these small volcanoes are scattered along the shores. It is sometimes said that the landscape looks like the mountains of the moon when viewed through a powerful telescope. Even more fantastic than these countless extinct volcanoes are the lava formations. When the lava was hot, it flowed down into the lake and made peninsulas and promontories. On the land it twisted itself into all sorts of strange shapes. There are caves and ravines and grottos, and at one place there are pillars and arches and towers which suggest ruined castles. In fact, it resembles them so much it is called Dark Castles.

From Myvatn you can see mountains which look as if the sun were always shining on them. These are patches of yellow sulphur. At one time sulphur was mined in this region and sold to foreign countries, but none is mined nowadays, for it does not sell for enough money to pay for the labor, the imported machinery and the shipping.

Besides the wild looking, squeegee lava forms such as surround Myvatn, there is another rocky form which is seen in many places, and which was also created by volcanoes and earthquakes. This has resulted from the flow of basalt. When the basalt was soft and hot, it seeped through a crack in the earth's surface, called a fissure, just as mud might seep through a crack between two boards. Gradually it cooled and hardened in long ridges and cliff-like walls which look as if they had been built by men. There are similar formations in the United States, such as the palisades along the Hudson River, in New York, but these are much older than those in Iceland. In fact, Iceland is the only country in the world where such basaltic flows, as they are called, are known to have occurred since human beings inhabited the globe. Although the basalt looks as if it might be good material for building, unfortunately it has proved unsuitable. Since there is practically no other kind of stone in the country or clay for making bricks, Iceland has to import not only all the wood that is needed in building, but also the bricks and cement. Of course, this makes houses, schools, churches, offices and every kind of building very expensive.

Every Icelandic boy and girl looks forward to taking a trip to Hekla and Myvatn. They also want to visit the hot springs and geysers. As you have learned, there are so many hot springs around Reykjavik that most of the buildings are heated with this natural hot water. There is another town about twenty-five miles from Reykjavik which is practically built on hot springs. The name of this town is Hveragerdi, but when the American soldiers were stationed in Iceland, they found this name so hard to pronounce that they called it Hurdy-Gurdy, and you can do the same.

There are so many hot springs there, with steam rising from them all the time, that the whole town seems to be enveloped in smoke. You may be interested to know that when the first settlers came to Iceland and saw such steam they named the place where they came ashore Reykjavik. Reykja means smoke. Vik means bay. So Reykjavik means Smoky Bay.

Wisps of this smoky steam float over Hveragerdi and there are great big greenhouses everywhere, using the heat from springs which we cannot see, but from which the hot water is piped. The flowers and vegetables which are raised in these greenhouses are sent to the markets in Reykjavik. Besides tomatoes and cucumbers, grapes and melons and bananas are raised here. Although they are very expensive, people buy all that grow. There are so many springs here that you can never tell when a new one is going to burst up suddenly through the ground. Sometimes one pops up almost under your feet, and gives you a surprise.

The biggest hot spring is not at Hveragerdi, but a good

deal further on. This is Great Geysir, which has given its name to all geysers in other countries. Great Geysir is on a plateau overlooking a winding river. When you reach the plateau, you will see a hotel and some sheep, an outdoor swimming pool and a greenhouse. A little distance away is a deep pool of clear water, in a basin about fifty feet across. Some steam is rising from it and this has a slight smell of sulphur.

Those travelers of long ago who had to journey to Great Geysir on pony back sometimes waited for days for it to spout, and then maybe returned without even having seen it in action. Nowadays, if a busload of people arrive and Geysir doesn't spout, there is a way to force the old fellow to wake up. A huge dose of soap is dumped into the basin. This forms a covering over the surface, compressing the steam. In a few moments Geysir gives a hiss and a growl and a roar, and up gushes a great column of steaming water, two hundred feet high. Out come the soap suds, like a burst of big, soft snowflakes, making the ground white before they disappear. Everyone exclaims, "AH!" in approval and then Geysir keeps on spouting for quite a few minutes, just for good measure— or perhaps to get rid of the nasty-tasting soap. By and by it stops and then the crowd breaks up and moves away to look at the other smaller geysers which dot the plateau. These little ones are really only bubbling hot springs.

Some dance like pretty fountains, flinging off spray and steam. Some gurgle gently and others under the ground cannot be seen at all. The only way you know they are there is because the ground above them is moist and warm and, if you listen, you can hear the water murmuring.

After you have looked at Great Geysir and the hot springs, you can go back to the hotel and have a swim in the outdoor pool with its warm water, and have dinner. You will probably be served salmon which has been caught that morning and cooked in the hot water which has been piped into the hotel from a near-by hot spring. There will be potatoes which have been dug from the garden and tomatoes which have been grown in the greenhouse. For dessert there will be a bowl of skyr with heavy cream—both of them furnished by the cows in the pasture.

Besides trips to see the geysers and hot springs, there are other enjoyable excursions to waterfalls. There are dozens of waterfalls in Iceland and nearly every one has its special admirers who insist that it is the one most worth seeing. However, there are three which are particularly famous—Gullfoss, Godafoss and Dettifoss,—(foss means fall) and these pour and thunder and dash and spray over their rims into the rocky chasms far below.

You remember reading that, because of the Gulf Stream, the harbors of Iceland never freeze, but there may sometimes be great blocks of ice drifting down from the Arctic seas, into the fjords. There is another place where there may be icebergs, even in summer, and this is the White Lake, in the central part of the country. Here a glistening white glacier stretches out two arms, down into the water, and every now and then there is a mighty crash as an iceberg breaks away from the glacier and floats on the surface of the lake. These icebergs are of curious shapes: they may be large or small and you can imagine that they are swans, or sailboats or castles or toy animals out of a fairy tale. When the sun shines on them, they flash and sparkle with all the colors of the rainbow.

Other excursions which are popular for boys and girls, as well as for grownups, are to various caves. There are many caves in Iceland. Along the south coast there are big ones which are sometimes used as stables and store-houses for hay. One of these has different levels of floors, just as if it had been built by men. Some of them have crosses cut in the walls, probably by Christians who lived in them a long time ago.

There is one cave named Surtshellir, which means the Giants' Cave. To get into it, you have to walk about a mile through a passage which winds underground, and is, of course, absolutely dark, or would be if you did not carry a light. The part of the cave which is most fascinating is where the floor is of solid ice. There are stalactites hanging down from the walls and ceiling and stalagmites rising up from the floor. When the beams from a flash-light strike them, they glitter and sparkle. There is a story that at one time eighteen young men ran away from the school where they were students and lived as outlaws in this cave. They took their sweethearts along with them for company, but in any case it must have been pretty uncomfortable in the cold and darkness.

There is still another place which is often visited. This is in the northern part of Iceland and is called Asbyrgi.

It is a huge, semicircular ravine, enclosed by very high, almost vertical cliffs. It reminds you of a football stadium for giants. There is a legend that the horse of the pagan god, Odin, made it with the pressure of his hoof. It is true that the shape of Asbyrgi is somewhat the shape of a horse's hoof, and that there is a big rock or island in the center which corresponds to the frog in a horse's hoof. In any case, this peaceful and beautiful ravine, protected from the wind by its high walls, is a fine place for camping. If you go there, you may see some white tents to prove that it is often used for this purpose.

Although the buses go to all these interesting places, there are people in Iceland who like to take long walking trips. They can always be sure of getting something to eat at any farm, and they enjoy seeing the wayside slowly and stopping when they please to look at a fine view.

Icelanders love their country, and although they are glad when tourists also come to know and love it, they themselves are the chief sightseers. From the time that they are children until they are old men and women, they spend their holidays visiting and admiring the strange and beautiful places.

## VII.    THE OLDEST PARLIAMENT
IN THE WORLD

ALL the places you read about in the last chapter are
interesting and some of them are very beautiful.
Icelanders enjoy taking trips to see them, still
there are people who have lived in Iceland all their lives
and have never been able to visit Hekla and Myvatn and
Great Geysir. There is, however, another place which

every Icelander is determined to see if possible, because it is in a special way the most important place in the whole country.

This is Thingvellir, and it holds somewhat the same position in the history of Iceland as Plymouth Rock and Jamestown hold in our history, for it was here that a republic was set up more than a thousand years ago—in the year 930.

This was a most unusual idea at that time. In fact, there had never been a republic before north of the Alps. All countries were governed by kings or emperors or rulers who had the power of life and death over their subjects.

The way it happened was this.

The Vikings who settled Iceland came from Norway because they did not want to live under a king who they thought was tyrannical. They wanted to make their own laws and govern themselves.

Soon after these first settlers had begun to cultivate their farms and build their houses of rock and turf, they built churches—one in each district. Such a church or temple was usually on the farm of some important man, who was not only the leading politician, but the priest of the temple as well. The temple was a meeting place for everyone in the district, and the people all gathered there to discuss whatever interested them.

By and by it occurred to the Icelanders that it would

be a good idea for all these separate groups, which were called Things, to meet together once a year in some central place and work out laws for the whole country. This big group would be called the Althing.

The Icelanders chose a man named Grimur Goatbeard to travel all around and find a suitable location for such a big group to meet and also to tell everyone about the coming event.

Grimur went up hill and down dale, through valleys and across mountains and finally decided on the valley which is today called Thingvellir. It is a wonderfully beautiful valley, very wide and green, lying between two high walls of cliffs. A river named Oxara winds through it and empties into a lake which is the largest, the deepest and one of the loveliest in the whole country.

Here, in the summer of 930, was established the Althing, and after that it met in this same valley every summer for more than eight hundred years. Every man of importance in his community came to the Althing, although in those days it was a long, rough journey which might take weeks for those who lived faraway. They came on pony back and on foot, fording streams and sleeping in the rain, and many of them brought their wives and children along with them.

When they reached the valley, there was plenty of grazing land for their ponies and plenty of room for everyone to camp out. Some of the chieftains built shelters for themselves—booths as they were called—with walls of rocks and roofs of woolen cloth, and they came back to these same booths every summer. Visitors can still see the outlines of the walls of some of these booths, and read the names, carved in stone, of the men who occupied them.

Behind the slope on which these booths were built, there is a high cliff of basalt. The Speaker stood on a stone in front of this wall, which acted as a sounding board, so that when he spoke all the people gathered in front of him—on the slope or in the valley—could hear him. The most important speaker was called a Lawman and he had to recite all the laws of Iceland. There were so many of these that it took him three summers to get through them. He also had to answer every legal question that was asked him.

The Althing decided matters concerning marriage, punishment for crimes, insurance against fire and many other things. It organized trial by jury three hundred years before this was even thought of in England.

The laws in Iceland were not only in advance of those in other countries at that time, but were in advance of the laws in many countries today. For instance, dueling was forbidden, and weights and measures were made the same throughout the country, and the prices of things bought and sold were fixed, so as to be fair to all. Punishments for those who broke the laws were swift and severe, but there was no such thing as torturing criminals.

The meeting of the Althing every summer was much more than a political occasion. It was a great festival, something like a fair and a national exhibition. Members of families who had moved away from home came to see their relatives again and to exchange news. Young people met and fell in love and their marriages were arranged. The men made plans for trips to foreign lands and listened to the stories of other men who had just returned from those lands.

There were games and sports, too. There is a flat-topped hill called the Maiden's Seat where the women and girls and children sat to look down on the men and boys wrestling.

This was a thousand years ago, but the valley and the cliffs, the lake and the river, the Maiden's Seat and the stones which mark where the Lawman stood and where the booths of the chieftains were built are still to be seen at Thingvellir. The Althing met here for 868 years. Then it was decided it would be more convenient to assemble in Reykjavik, under a roof, instead of in this remote valley, under the open sky. So after that, the Althing met in the city, and today it holds its sessions in a handsome building, with plenty of room for the two chambers, which are like the United States Senate and House of Representatives.

At one time, when Iceland was under Danish domination, it had to give up the Althing for a while. Then it was restored, so it may now be called the oldest parliament in the world.

As has already been mentioned more briefly, the way Iceland came under Danish rule was like this.

After the Althing was established, and the laws were drawn up, the people realized that no provision had been made as to how the laws were to be enforced. It was something like our UN, which can recommend ways to act, but cannot make people act that way if they do not want to. The individual priest-chieftains, who had been so powerful and independent before the Althing had been organized, still wanted to hold on to their old power. They quarreled so much among themselves that, as you learned in Chapter II, it finally seemed best to ask Norway to help them settle their disputes and keep the peace. It ended up with Norway gaining control of Iceland, and later with Denmark taking over that control. These were hard years for Iceland, and she was unhappy and poor. It was not until the Second World War that she finally regained her independence and became prosperous and happy.

The Althing met again in Thingvellir for old times'

*Medallion struck to celebrate Republic of Iceland*

sake in June, 1944, and declared Iceland a republic. Two years later Iceland became a member of the UN.

So today Iceland is a republic, just as the United States is a republic. It has a president, who is elected for four years, and four political parties. It has its own money and its own flag and stamps. This flag has a bright blue background, with a red and white cross placed lengthwise on it. It is beautiful when you see it rippling against the blue sky of Iceland. The stamps show pictures of Hekla and Geysir and other famous places and those which carry the designs of fish are among the prettiest in the world.

The boys and girls in Iceland now take all these things more or less for granted, just as American boys and girls take their form of government for granted. But they dearly love to visit Thingvellir, and on holidays or over week ends during the summer there are often forty or fifty white tents pitched along the river. The visitors may hire boats and go fishing in the lake or they may prefer to stroll around, looking at the places where the chieftains once had their booths and where the Lawman stood when he recited the laws to the people, and at the waterfalls and splendid views.

Many of the cliffs look like the profiles of men and have their names and legends. Around the rim of the lake there is quite a settlement of summer houses, a hotel and a new church and parsonage. These last two follow the old-fashioned lines and style of their ancient predecessors. There is even turf on the three gabled roofs of the parsonage, to make it like the previous dwellings which stood there centuries ago.

In 1930, Thingvellir was made into a National Park, so it will always be preserved. Trees are being planted and no sheep are permitted to graze there, because they would nibble the young trees and destroy them.

Thingvellir is a popular place for conventions and

other big affairs to be held.

Today no criminals in Iceland are put to death, but in the early days there were swift, terrible punishments for wrong-doers. Thus at Thingvellir you can see a cleft between two crags where murderers were hanged, and a deep pool where women who had sinned were drowned, and another place where heretics were burned.

The story about these heretics is interesting.

The men who colonized Iceland were pagans because Norway, where they had been born, was still a pagan land, believing in weather gods. The most powerful god was Odin, who was the Father of Time. The Norwegians believed that he had two black ravens which during the day flew all over the world, and at night returned to tell him what they had seen and heard. His wife Frigga had a dress made of falcon feathers and when she put it on she could fly anywhere. Another god was Thor, who was the god of war.

There were many of these pagan gods and goddesses, and some of them the people loved and some they disliked and some they were afraid of.

About the time the Althing was established, people in Iceland began to hear more and more about a wonderful new religion called Christianity. They talked and argued about it, and finally, in the year 1000, there was a great discussion in Thingvellir as to whether the country

71

as a whole should give up its heathen gods and adopt the White Christ.

By and by it was decided to turn the matter over to the Lawman. For three days and three nights he sat in his booth, with a sheepskin pulled over his head, so he would not be distracted by the sun which shines all through the night in summer. Finally he left his booth and climbed up to the rock and stood on it and told the crowd waiting to hear him that hereafter everyone should worship the White Christ.

The people agreed to this, but when they were told they must be baptized in the river or lake, they refused. They said the water was too cold. Finally someone had the bright idea of going to some hot springs and being baptized there. This suited people much better and they all trooped off and were baptized.

From this you can see that it wasn't really a great religious conversion with all the people, but chiefly a matter of convenience. For a long while the Icelanders kept to some of their heathen practices, while also following Christian ones. There were, of course, some who were not so lukewarm. There was one nobleman, for instance, who had become a Christian and was extremely eager to convert other people. He took the images of his heathen gods and threw them into a rushing waterfall, so everyone could see that he was discarding them. The name of that waterfall is Godafoss, which means the waterfall of the gods, and if you ever go to Myvatn, you will pass it on the way and can see it without getting out of the car or bus. It is not a very high waterfall, but it is one of the prettiest in Iceland and its name reminds us of the time when the whole country was a heathen land.

Speaking of Christianity, as you now know, even before the first Vikings came to Iceland, some monks had come there from Ireland. These monks wanted to find a place where they could meditate and pray and not be distracted. Since there were no other people in the whole country of Iceland, it suited them very well. However, they had not been there very long before the Vikings arrived. The Vikings were heathens and the monks were either unwilling to live beside them as neighbors or were afraid of them. In any case, they got out as soon as they could. Some of them went to an island off the east coast of Iceland named Papey from the Latin word "papa," which means bishop. The Westman Islands, which you will read about later in this book, were also named for these refugees, for they were called Men of the West (West Men).

When we speak of the first colonizers, we do not mean these monks, for they made no attempt to build homes and raise families and establish a colony. All they left behind them when they fled were a few bells and crosses.

But the Vikings did not forget where these monks had originally come from and when they needed some slaves, they would sail down to Ireland and capture men and women. They did this so often that there are quite a few people in Iceland today with Irish blood, which often shows itself in the dark hair, unlike the Norse yellow hair.

After Iceland had become Christianized, churches were built, with paintings, carvings, statues and embroideries depicting, not Odin and Thor and all the other pagan gods, but St. Peter and St. Paul, the Virgin Mary and the Christ Child.

For about five hundred years the Icelanders were Roman Catholics and during this time the monks were busy translating and copying books and also teaching the people to read and write. If it had not been for them, many things would have been lost which are now preserved in Icelandic museums.

Lutheranism later became the state religion of Iceland and has remained so ever since. There is a Lutheran Cathedral in Reykjavik and there are Lutheran churches throughout the country. A Lutheran bishop is called Herra and a Lutheran minister is called Sira, and these are the only honorary titles left in Iceland, for the Icelanders are extremely democratic and believe that everyone is as good as everyone else. They express this feeling of equality by usually calling one another by the first name, instead of using Mr. or Mrs. or Miss.

Although the Lutheran Church is the only one supported by the State, anyone can follow any religion he chooses and worship when and where and how he chooses. This is what is called religious freedom, which anyone certainly does not practice when he feels any prejudice against people because of their religion.

Thingvellir is the place to hear about these things.

Americans sometimes find it hard to believe that hundreds of years before their country was discovered, Iceland had its well-run parliament meetings in this wide green valley. Reykjavik looks like a new city because most of the buildings are new. It is only when you go to Thingvellir that you realize that the country is really very old. For here was established the oldest republic which exists in the world. It is not only because of its great age, but because of its wise laws that we admire that republic, for many far larger and far richer countries are just beginning to learn now some of the things Iceland knew and practiced a thousand years ago.

## VIII.  RICHES FROM THE SEA

I F, instead of looking at Iceland from an automobile
or a plane, you could go around it in a glass-
bottomed boat, you would see a million fish darting
through the water. You know how thick a swarm of mosquitoes can be at certain times and places. Well, the fish
in Icelandic waters at certain seasons can be just as
thick.

There are many different kinds of fish—but it is principally cod and herring that are caught at different seasons in different places. Thus January and February, April and May are the months for codfish off the shores of the Westman Islands and from July to September is the time for herring on the north coast. Then the fishermen are so busy they hardly have time to sleep.

Most of the codfish is caught by line fishing. Such a line may be as much as ten miles long, with ten thousand hooks on it, each attached to the line by a string. It takes many men many hours to attach these hooks to the line and to bait each one of them with a little piece of herring. When this is done, the line is thrown overboard from the trawler and the codfish swarm to the bait. By and by the line must be pulled in and all the hooks that have codfish on them are torn off. The fish are taken off the hooks and new hooks tied on the line and baited with more herring. In winter weather this is a cold, hard job for the fishermen, but they may make enough money to make it well worth their while. Not only do Icelandic boats gather around this region, but trawlers and motorboats and steam transports come from England, Norway, Sweden, Denmark and France.

The same thing is true in the summer, when the herring swarm into the fjords in the northern part of the country. These are often caught by huge nets which are dropped into the water from a big boat. Sometimes one single boat may pull out two thousand barrels of herring in ten minutes. In a good year, more herring is caught off the coast of Iceland than off the coasts of the United States and Alaska combined.

Now, you may wonder what in the world a country as small as Iceland can do with so much fish. To be sure, almost everybody eats fish every day at some meal. Every Icelandic girl knows how to pick out a fish which is absolutely fresh and how to cook it so that it is sweet and juicy and firm. But if all the people in Iceland ate fish and nothing but fish, they could hardly eat up all that is caught. Therefore the fish which they do not use is sold to other countries.

You remember reading that Iceland has no wood which can be used for building, and no metals, and has to import practically everything it uses except farm products, such as mutton, milk, butter, wool and leather. In order to pay for all the household things she needs— in order to buy automobiles and telephones, paper and pencils, tools and medicines, she herself has to produce something she can sell or trade in exchange. Fish is the only thing she can raise and sell abroad. So you see how important it is for her to catch lots of fish—far more than 130,000 people could eat.

The Icelandic fish is not only plentiful, but it is especially delicious, and also extremely nutritious. The only difficulty about selling it abroad is that, unless it is promptly and properly treated, it spoils very quickly.

However, there are many ways of preserving fish so it will keep a long time. In the early days, the codfish was caught, split open and cleaned and then laid out in the sun and wind to dry. When it was perfectly dry and hard and white, it was stacked up in great piles and shipped to Spain and South America and other places. Nowadays more codfish is dried by artificial means than by the wind and sun. Some is salted, some is made into codliver oil and there is always a good sale for this. Some is packed in ice, when it is caught and the boat carrying it goes directly to England or the continent.

We think of codfish in the south of Iceland and herring in the north.

It is great fun to go to a village on the north coast named Siglufordur, and see the herring being brought ashore. The catch must be unloaded gently into wicker baskets, so that it will not be bruised, and then it is carried to the salting station in shallow, high-legged push trucks running on tracks. These are lifted from the trucks into long troughs, from which the salter, who is frequently a girl, lifts out each one by hand. She cleans and cuts it, rolls it in salt and packs it in barrels with more salt. No herring which is more than six to eight hours old is permitted to be salted—and this is one reason why they are so good.

Besides being salted, herring may be dried, smoked, spiced, pickled—in fact, there seems to be no end to the ways it can be prepared. Whatever is not used for food is used in some other way. Its oil is used in making soap, and margarine, and for medicine. If any part is left over, it is ground into a meal, which is fed to cattle.

Drying and salting and pickling and smoking fish have been done for years in Iceland. But recently a new method has been introduced. This is quick freezing, and in this Iceland is far ahead of any other country in Europe. There are quick freezing plants all up and down the coasts—about sixty of them.

When the fish is brought into port, it is carried out of the boats directly into the factory by a mechanical conveyor. It is quickly cleaned and cut into proper sized pieces, which are called fillets, and packed in parchment paper for Europe and in cardboard boxes for the United States. These are clapped into the freezers, and in an hour and a half each one is a solid block. When these are sent away on refrigerator ships, they arrive at their destination still frozen. There may be a canning factory in the same building with the quick freezing machinery. Recently there have been some experiments in shipping fish by plane.

There are two reasons why the Icelandic frozen fish taste so good. First it is because the fish themselves are

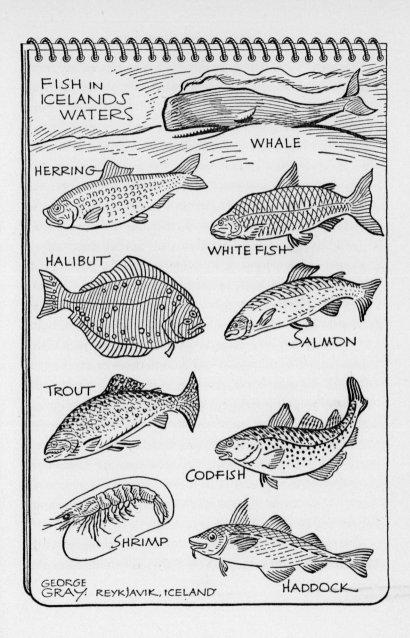

FISH IN ICELANDS WATERS

WHALE

HERRING

WHITE FISH

HALIBUT

SALMON

TROUT

CODFISH

SHRIMP

HADDOCK

GEORGE GRAY. REYKJAVIK, ICELAND

fat and firm. Second, it is against the law to freeze any fish which is more than forty-eight hours old. Most of it is only twenty-four hours old, for usually a fishing boat goes out one evening and is back the next evening.

Iceland is extremely proud of her fishing products and takes the greatest care to protect the places where the young fish are growing up. About a fifth of the people in Iceland make their living from something to do with fish. Many others make part of their living that way, such as the University students who may spend their summer vacations working on herring trawlers.

While cod and herring are the principal fish in the waters around Iceland, there are many others, such as white fish, haddock, and halibut. While there are no shell fish, such as lobsters, oysters or clams, there is a tiny shrimp which is very good and is sometimes canned.

Besides the fish in the salt water, there is a wealth of fish in the rivers, ponds and lakes. First there is salmon, and it is such fun to catch this that anglers come from the British Isles and even from Canada and the United States for the sport. While the salmon are plentiful enough for everyone to have it for dinner during the season, there is not enough to freeze for export, like the cod and the herring. If a fisherman catches fifteen salmon in an afternoon, he may take a few home for supper and carry the rest to a factory where they will smoke them or can them for his winter use. The trout is also delicious, and some of this is canned in tasty sauces and spices. There are other fish which are sought out by anglers and which, although they may not be caught in large enough numbers to be exported, give variety to the local markets.

Long ago fishing used to be a terribly hard, disagreeable and even a dangerous occupation. At first there were only open rowboats and the fishermen had to catch the fish with fishing lines. They did not dare venture far out to sea, but stayed in the fjords and near the shores. By and by they got decked sailing vessels, and these could go farther and stay out longer. Just before 1900, the first experiments were made with steam trawlers, and then with motorboats. Nowadays great steam trawlers costing nearly half a million dollars apiece go out in all weathers. The men have comfortable, dry quarters and all kinds of machinery to lower the nets and bring them up again with their tons of squirming silver herring.

Even with all these improvements, there is still plenty of hard work on a fishing vessel. In winter the boats used in fishing for cod are supposed to be at sea only twenty-four hours from the time they leave shore until they return. But often they are caught in rough weather and the men have to stay out much longer than that. Some years there may not be enough herring, and then the fishermen do not make much money. Another year one small boat may take in 3000 tons in the three months' season.

The government does everything it possibly can to improve fishing conditions, to protect the fish and to help the fishermen. Among other things, it sends out tiny Gruman boats, which are small aquaplanes. These go skimming above the water, looking down to see where a dark patch would indicate a school of herring. When such a school is sighted, the news and the location are flashed by radio to boats in the region. These then hurry directly to the place, and so save the time and fuel that might have been used in searching around.

These Gruman planes are so small that when they land in a harbor of a town, they taxi right up into it and park alongside the main street as easily as a jeep.

Sometimes the herring refuse to bite. When this happens, a town like Sigulfordur is very much upset. There it has all its machinery for salting and smoking and spicing. It has its factories and driers. Thousands of buyers and speculators and great gangs of workmen have come from faraway. In the harbor are boats from many countries. Everything is going full blast, with smoke from the furnaces and driers rising into the sky twenty hours a day. Then the herring decide they won't be caught! Everyone in Iceland is terribly worried. The first thing they look for in the newspapers and the first thing they listen to on the radio is how the herring are behaving or misbehaving.

The fishermen in Sigulfordur may have nothing to do and sleep all day. Then suddenly a school of herring is sighted and the news is flashed forth. The fishermen tumble out of bed, even if it is in the middle of the night. The girls and women in the salting sheds take their turns at sleeping and working, for the preserving must go on at top speed as long as the herring are being brought in.

Thus you see that fish and fishing affect the life of everyone in Iceland. If the people of Iceland could not sell fish to other countries, they could not buy anything from those countries. Whether a boy gets a bicycle for Christmas or a girl gets a doll's tea set may all depend on whether there has been a good herring season.

A fisherman is as respected in Iceland as a doctor or a lawyer and the owner of a fishing vessel may be a good deal richer than a professional or business man.

If you will look at the Icelandic postage stamps, you will see on many of them a graceful picture of a fish. This is quite suitable for a country which makes its living from the water, as much as from the land.

IX.                                                    CO-OPS

T**HE** Icelanders have a way of buying and selling
which is extremely sensible and makes or saves
money for everyone. This is the system of cooperatives, called co-ops for short.

In order to understand what a co-op is, let us suppose
you think it would be fun to play "keeping store." Perhaps you have saved a dollar and you buy twenty pieces
of candy at five cents each. You take a table or a board

for a counter and arrange the candy and charge seven cents for each piece. You invite the other children to come in and they buy all your candy. When you count your money, you have $1.40 instead of one dollar, for you have made two cents on each of the twenty pieces. You have earned that forty cents because you saved your dollar and took the time and trouble to buy the candy and arrange it in a convenient place and call in the other boys and girls. You yourself did not make the candy and you did not eat it. You bought it from one person and sold it to another, and you were, therefore, what is called a middleman.

This is the way most stores and shops in the United States are run. Each one is run independently by a middleman, who buys the groceries or tools or whatever he may handle in large quantities and sells them in smaller quantities and makes money on each article.

About seventy years ago a group of farmers in Iceland got together. They decided what things they needed, such as fertilizer and tools, and then they all put in money to buy these in one big lot and secured the fertilizer and tools more cheaply because they bought them in quantity. Later they started a store where they could buy these things at a cheaper price. When they sold them, they themselves got the profits, instead of their going to a middleman, because each farmer had put in money and was a part owner.

This little group of farmers in Iceland started a co-op and soon lots of other little groups sprang up all over the country. Today there are fifty-five co-ops in Iceland. Each of them elects its manager and board of directors. Most of them belong to a large central organization, or Federation, and they choose one or more of its members to represent it at the Federation Congress which meets once a year.

Now although the first co-ops started with farmers who got together in a group so that they could buy things together and distribute them without a middleman, very soon they realized the advantages of a co-op not only in buying, but in selling.

For instance, the very same farmer who has bought his fertilizer and tools through a co-op has milk to sell. He can take it to a dairy and get paid ten cents a quart for it. The dairy distributes it to its customers for fifteen cents a quart. In other words, the dairy is the middleman, and makes a profit of five cents a quart. Or the farmer can take his own horse and cart or his automobile and go around from house to house and sell his milk directly to his customers. His wife can make butter and cheese and he can take this with him and sell it. This takes a good deal of time and means he has to keep a horse or a car.

The third way the farmer can sell his milk is through

a co-op. If he is a member of such a group all he does is to put his milk in big tin cans at the entrance to his farm. By and by a truck which is owned by the co-op comes and picks it up and takes it to the nearest town. Here there is a co-op dairy, which separates the milk from the cream and makes cheese and butter and skyr, which is that delicious food something like cottage cheese. The dairy then sends these products to a milk shop—which may or may not be owned by a co-op. People come to this shop with their own pitchers and buy the milk and carry it home. Now the milk is probably cheaper than if it had gone through the hands of a middleman, and that is an advantage to the customer. Also at the end of the year whatever profits have been made are divided among all the members of the co-op. Since the farmer who sold the milk is a member, he gets a per cent of the profits. If the customer who bought the milk is a member of the co-op, he also shares in the profits.

While the co-ops in Iceland started with the farmers, their membership now includes fishermen and merchants and manufacturers and housekeepers.

When the time comes for rounding up the sheep, those which the farmer does not need for food or wool, he takes to a co-op slaughtering house. The meat is sold to a co-op butcher and the wool is washed in a co-op cleaning plant. Then it may be sold to a co-op textile mill to be made

89

into cloth. There are co-op shoe factories which use the coarser skins, and glove and bag factories which use the finer ones.

All these things are sold in co-op shops. Anyone, whether or not they are members, can buy in these shops, but if you are a member you will get your share of profits at the end of the year.

Co-ops handle other things beside food. A co-op may build an apartment house or private homes or a hotel. Those who rent accommodations in such buildings not only find them cheaper than buildings which are independently owned and handled through a middleman, but at the end of the year they receive a share of the profits. In Akureyri, which is the largest town in the north, there is a very attractive hotel which was built and is owned and run by a co-op. Not only members but anyone can engage a room or buy a meal there, but there again, the members have this advantage. Whatever profits there are at the end of the year are divided among them.

Co-ops exist in many, many countries besides Iceland. There are a good many in the United States and Canada. But in Iceland you are very conscious of them because they handle so very many things.

Just as the farmer buys and sells through a co-op, so does the fishermen. His boat may be co-operatively owned, and his fish salted or smoked or frozen and sold

GEORGE
GRAY
ICELAND

through a co-op. In every case, the things are cheaper because there is no middleman.

Anyone can join a co-op. It makes no difference what his politics are or what his religion is or whether he is a member of a union or not. Anyone can get out whenever he pleases.

The co-ops run a school in Reykjavik, which gives a two-year training course for positions in the society. They also run a correspondence school.

One reason co-ops are so successful in Iceland is because all the people in the country have gone to the same kind of school and church and have pretty much the same ideas. They can get a group together and then can agree on what that group wants to do. In the United States there are people of many different races, and with different ideas. Also one part of the United States is very different from another part and produces different things. Some of these regions do not feel the need of organizing

91

co-ops, but would rather do things independently.

But it is interesting to see how sensibly Iceland co-ops work and how they help practically everyone to save money whether they are buying or selling or simply shopping in a co-op store.

## X.  SOME BIRDS AND ANIMALS IN ICELAND

THERE is not a zoo in all Iceland. This means that the boys and girls there—unless they have traveled abroad to some other country—have never seen a lion or an elephant or a tiger or any such animals, as boys and girls in the United States can see in a zoo. Even if there were a zoo in Iceland, the people might not enjoy it, for they do not like to think of animals in cages or in captivity of any kind.

You have read about the animals on a farm: the sheep, ponies, cows, cats, dogs, poultry and pigs. The Icelanders are kind to these animals and teach the children to be, too. On some farms, foxes and mink are raised for their fur, and these, of course, have to be kept in enclosures, so they cannot kill the chickens and lambs.

There are not many wild animals. In one place in the north there is a herd of reindeer. The first of these were brought from Norway a long time ago (1771) and the Icelanders hoped they would become much more numerous and give them meat and milk and leather as they do in Norway. But although the herd did increase, it has never become large enough to be valuable. These deer roam as they please and at certain seasons hunters are permitted to kill a few for food.

Since there are no forests—or at least what we mean by forests—naturally there is no place for such animals as can live only in woods and jungles. And since it is never really hot, there are no animals such as must have a tropical climate. However, there are miles of coast line where seals love to sun themselves on the rocks. The seals are very playful and love to chase the salmon far up into the fjords and to follow passing boats, especially if they can see a bit of bright color or hear strains of music.

There are enough whales in not too distant waters to

BIRDS AND ANIMALS
IN ICELAND by GEORGE
GRAY
ICELAND

RAVEN

SHEEP

COMORANT

THE
FAITHFUL
PONY

BEAR

PTARMIGAN

REINDEER

FOX

SEA GULL

SEAL

MINK

keep a whaling factory busy. In the old days, all that was used of a great whale was its blubber or fat. But nowadays every particle is valuable. The oil can be refined and used to make soap and margarine. The meat is used for food for domestic animals, the bones are ground up to make fertilizer. Certain explosives are made with whale oil, and some machinery requires sperm oil for lubrication.

Sometimes, from Polar waters a bear comes floating to shore on a block of ice, and this is regarded with the greatest curiosity by the seals as well as by the people.

There are not, you see, many kinds of wild animals, but there are many kinds of birds. While two kinds of penguins are said to be found, the third and strangest kind has now disappeared entirely. This was the great Auk, which stood as high as a man. Today no Icelander would go out and shoot a harmless animal for sport, but at the time when there were great Auks, men were not educated as they are now. They killed so many Auks that soon there were only a few left. These found an island, named Eldey, off the west coast and thought they would be safe there. But a volcano on the island erupted and that finished the Auk colony—so now there are only pictures and printed descriptions to tell us about these huge, strange creatures.

But although there are not any more great Auks, there are plenty of other sea birds. In fact, in some places there seem to be as many birds in the air as there are fish in the sea. There are different kinds of ducks, such as the mallard, the widgeon, the pin tail, Barrow's Golden Eye, etc. They lay their eggs on narrow ledges, along steep bare cliffs that face the sea. The wind may make the eggs roll around, but they are shaped in such a way they don't blow off. These eggs are considered delicious and bring a good price in the market at Reykjavik. They are gathered in this way. A man is let down by rope from the top of the cliff and he dangles there between the sky and the sea, while he collects as many eggs as he can carry. When he wants to catch the birds for food, he goes down by means of a rope, carrying a kind of net at the end of a long pole. When the birds rise from the ledges to fly, he very skillfully catches them in the net and kills them at once.

There are millions of gulls and sometimes when they are startled and fly out from their nests, it is as though a dark curtain were being drawn across the sky.

There is one duck which is extremely valuable and which is protected by law. This is the eider duck.

They like to nest in the same place, year after year, and farmers do not disturb them, but do everything they can to attract them. Since these birds love bright colors and glittery objects they can be lured to a place by mirrors, tinsel and flags. When the mother duck has made her

97

nest, she plucks the down from her breast to line it. This down is the softest, warmest down in all the world, and the Icelanders love to use it in those down puffs, which you read about in chapter 3. They can always be sure of selling it abroad for a good price, if they have more than they need at home.

The father duck is called a drake and is much handsomer than the mother.

The father and mother mate for life and are very devoted. While she is laying her small, olive green eggs, he stands beside her and makes encouraging sounds, and she answers him with affectionate quacks. While she is hatching the eggs, he goes off with the other drakes. But he returns to his wife later. The mother works hard to take care of her little brood. She may weigh as much as eleven pounds when she begins sitting on the eggs, but when she leads her ducklings to the sea for their first swim, she may be down to less than half that. When the ducklings have left the nest, these nests are collected for the precious down.

There are other water birds, which live not on the sea, but in inland lakes and ponds. The swan is the handsomest and largest of these. There are a great many of them in Iceland and they look extremely beautiful with their graceful bodies and glitteringly white feathers, rocking on the blue surface of a lake. They make their nests on piles of twigs and waterplants, and when the baby swans or cygnets are small, the mother is so fierce as to be dangerous if any one bothers her or them.

When the swans fly, they form in a wedged shaped flock, each flock led by one of the oldest of them. As they lift themselves from the water and fly with outstretched necks, they are as beautiful against the blue sky as they were against the blue water. Although they fly rapidly— for their wings may measure six or seven feet from tip to tip, they do not ever seem to hurry. They trumpet in a strange, wild song, the sounds varying from deepest bass to a falsetto.

No one would ever think of killing a swan, although sometimes they become so numerous that they destroy the farmers' fields. In the old days, the stiff, white tail feathers used to be picked up and the base sharpened into a point. This made the quill pens with which old letters and books used to be written. Sometimes you can see such quill pens for sale even today and often you can see them in pictures of old times.

There are many birds which come to Iceland in the summer to nest and lay their eggs, and in the fall they fly back home. That home may be thousands of miles away —in Greece or in North Africa or even on the American east coast. The graceful tern spends its winters in the Antarctic and flies 25,000 miles every year so that it can enjoy the midnight sun at opposite ends of the world. People say that it always returns to Iceland precisely on March tenth, and this marks the beginning of summer. The routes they follow are like those taken by airplanes.

No one kills such birds for sport, although there is one which is shot for food. This is the ptarmigan, which is a stocky bird like a grouse, and builds its nest on the moors and open fields. Its plumage blends so softly with the gray and brown lichens and mosses that you can sometimes look directly at it without noticing it. In the winter this plumage becomes pure white like the snow and protects it from its enemies.

There are so many land and water birds in Iceland that you would get tired if you had to read all their names and a description of their habits and plumage. But there are three more which you will want to hear about. The first is the white tailed eagle. There are not many of these, but sometimes you can see one sitting beside a stream, watching for a salmon or a trout. When they start to fly, they seem clumsy and heavy, but once in the air they soar gloriously.

The most romantic of all the Icelandic birds is the falcon. This is the largest of the hawk family and it may be three feet when it is standing. While there are many kinds of falcons or hawks, the Icelandic falcon used to be considered one of the most famous and valuable, and it

GEORGE
GRAY
ICELAND

was chosen by kings and noblemen in a sport called falconry.

The falcon was caught when it was very young and carefully trained to sit upon the wrist of the man who had trained it, and to be carried out to the fields to hunt other birds. Since a falcon can fly almost 150 miles an hour, and can fly 500 miles without stopping, you can see how swift it is. It is also very powerful. When it sees another bird it wants to kill for food, it drops down out of the sky like lightning, stuns it with its beak, and then, before the helpless bird can drop, the falcon clutches it in its claws.

When falconry was a royal sport in England and on

the continent in Shakespeare's time, there were men who made a business of training falcons to pursue other birds, and then not to devour them, but to bring them back to their masters. Their hearing is extremely keen. They might be so far up in the sky that they could not be seen, but when their master whistled, they would hear it and come back instantly.

The Icelandic falcon was found to be one of the best for the sport, and at one time the King of Denmark issued orders that he alone should have the falcons caught in Iceland and he used to send a ship there just for the purpose of bringing the birds back to Denmark.

This royal sport is not often practiced today, except in the Orient. But the falcon is not forgotten in Iceland. There is an order, or society, called the Order of the Icelandic Falcon. It is the only order in Iceland. The President of Iceland is the Grand Master and he may confer the honor of membership on either men or women, Icelanders or foreigners. There are four classes: The Grand Cross, Grand Knight with a Star, Grand Knight and Knight. The size and design of insignia of each of these four classes are different, but they all show a gold or silver falcon against a background of Icelandic blue.

The third bird which may interest you is the big, black, glossy raven. This is like our crow but larger, and may measure four feet from wing tip to wing tip. It is

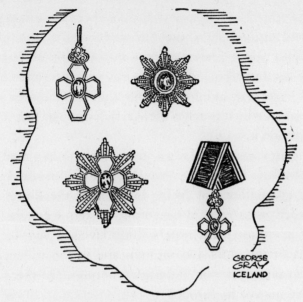

*Order of Icelandic Falcon*

very fond of being near people. Wherever you see a farmer ploughing or sheep grazing or ponies playing, you may see a raven or two hopping near by. It is a saucy impudent sort of bird, and sometimes is accused of being even worse. Farmers declare that sometimes a raven will attack a baby lamb and pick out its eyes, and older people believe that when someone lies dying in a house, the ravens know it and gather above the house cawing.

These unkind reports about their habits do not bother the sociable creatures. People may not like them, but they

103

like people. In the winter a male and female raven pair off, and a pair settles at each farmhouse.

About twenty miles off the north coast of Iceland there lies a small island named Grimsey. It is only about three miles long and half as wide, and it is the only part of Iceland which touches the Arctic circle. In fact it lies directly on it.

Grimsey is covered with grass, without any trees or even bushes. There aren't many people on this island, but there are millions of birds. In summer the shores are crowded with eider duck, terns, oysters catchers, red sand pipers and many others. Gulls lay their eggs on the ledges of the cliffs. On the hills and in the valleys are golden plover, dunlin and snow buntings. On the pools are red necked phalaropes.

There are funny looking puffins with red and orange bills. With this bill they like to dig long burrows on the top of the cliffs, and inside the bill, stuffed away in what looks like an elastic rosette in the corner, they can carry a dozen small fish.

The birds love Grimsey because they are not disturbed by human beings. There is plenty to eat and during the summer, there is light all night long. Before the cold, dark, windy winter sets in, almost all of them leave for warmer countries faraway.

But the people of Grimsey stay right there. Even if

during the gales and storms of winter, they are almost cut off from the mainland, they are content. They are fond of playing chess, and have plenty of time for it. An American named Willard Fiske, who was an expert chess player, was so impressed by their skill in this game that he gave them a small library.

Sometimes we make the mistake of thinking that birds are found only where there are trees. There certainly are very few trees in Iceland, but there are plenty of birds. In the cities, pigeons nest in corners of buildings and hop in the streets. In the country, the ravens prance in the ploughed fields and the ptarmigan and golden plover and the whimbrel nest on the moors. The eider duck settles in big colonies near friendly farms and on the inland lakes float swans and ducks. Falcons and eagles soar up into the sky. And along the coast and from the ledges of the cliffs that face the water, millions of other birds scream and dart back and forth and lay their eggs on narrow ledges where they rock and roll, but do not fall off even in a gale.

An artist in Reykjavik named Gudmundur Einarsson has modeled many of these birds and animals you have read about in this chapter. These little statues, about life size and accurately colored, are popular in Iceland and have been sent to museums all over the world.

So although there is no zoo in the country and although

there are only a few wild animals, there seems to be enough motion from whirring wings and enough sound from cawing and whistling throats to give color and liveliness to Iceland.

GEORGE
GRAY

## XI.    OLD WORDS, OLD STORIES
AND OLD AND NEW BOOKS

THERE is a group of countries in Europe called
Scandinavian. These countries are Norway and
Sweden, Denmark and Iceland. Frequently Fin-
land is included in the list, for it was part of Sweden for
more than six hundred years.

A long time ago, before Iceland was discovered, the

inhabitants of all of the Scandinavian countries spoke the Norse language. It was not precisely the same in the different nations, but it was similar enough for all Scandinavians to be able to understand one another.

When the Norwegians settled in Iceland, they, of course, spoke Norse, as they had at home. And the Icelanders still speak it. It has changed somewhat in the course of time, but not very much. If one of the first colonists should come back to Reykjavik, he would be able to understand what people were saying. If he had been able to read Norse a thousand years ago, he could read an Icelandic newspaper today. The difference between old Norse and present-day Icelandic is not as great as that between the English in Shakespeare's plays and the language we speak today.

Incidentally, a great many words in the English language came from Norse, and in Iceland you will see and hear such words all the time. A few examples will show you how similar these words are to ours. The Norse (or Icelandic) word for spoon is spónn. Ágúst means August. Bak is back. Their hey is our hay. Kol is coal. Hús is house, bók is book, heim is home, tún is town. Icelandic líf is life: postcard is póstkort, persóna is person, pappir is paper.

These are just a few of the many words which the English language has borrowed from the Norse.

As has been said, all the Scandinavians could understand one another a thousand years ago. Then certain differences began to creep in within the different countries. By and by it was not so easy for a Swede to understand a Dane or a Dane to understand a Norwegian. In parts of Finland people began to speak a language which nobody else could understand at all. But the Icelanders kept right on speaking Norse. Not enough foreigners came to the faraway, small country to bring in new words. Today, other Scandinavians cannot understand Icelandic because their languages have changed in a thousand years and Icelandic has remained very much as it was.

Icelanders have always been very proud of their language. In those dreadful years which are called the Dark Ages, when there were so many volcanic eruptions and diseases and famines, all they possessed was their history and literature. Even if a man had no money and not enough food or clothes and his house was miserable and falling down, he was able to tell himself and his neighbors precisely who his great, great grandfather was; where he lived and what he did and when he died and how many children he left and what their names were, for from the very first the settlers kept an exact record of every single family. Those records have been preserved carefully down to today, which means that Iceland has an unbroken account of its history.

Besides these records, the Icelanders had their stories, their legends and their laws. They honored and preserved these and handed them down from father to child.

As we have said, few foreigners came to Iceland in those early years—in fact, it was not until the Second World War that many foreigners had ever seen this island so far north. But the Icelanders went to other countries. They went because they had to do business with other people—to sell their fish and furs and leather and feathers and wool, and to buy things they needed, such as grain, lumber, metals and tools. They also went because they loved to visit foreign places.

The younger men of the best families often had an opportunity to make such business trips. They traveled to England and Norway, to France, Italy, Germany, Russia and the Orient and they learned about life in these places. When they came back home, there was a lot to tell about the way other people lived, and their families and friends loved to gather and listen to their accounts.

The young Icelanders who were most successful on their business trips abroad were those who could make up poetry quickly and cleverly. They were called Skalds, and an accomplished Skald could stand before the throne of a foreign king and compose verses on any subject the king commanded. Often the kings admired these Skalds so much they gave them titles and money.

When the Skalds returned to their homeland they brought back all sorts of information. Of course, there were no radios in those days and no newspapers. All news was given out by word of mouth and it was not until long afterward that a great deal of it was written down. In the confusion of wars and disasters in other countries, bits of information and records were lost, like pieces in a picture puzzle when the table is overturned. But many of these fragments were preserved in the verses of the Skalds and centuries later they have been fitted into the picture. This is one reason why skaldic poetry is valuable.

But at the time when the Skalds stood up and recited their long poems to their families, friends and neighbors, the information was only half the enjoyment. The other half was in the game of making up the verses.

These had to rhyme in a certain complicated way, the emphasis had to fall on certain syllables, and there were so many strict rules the Skald had to follow that it is hard to believe he could make up his verses as he went along and not break any of the rules. It was almost like playing several games of anagrams at the same time and doing it all in your head without any printed letters.

It is also hard to believe that practically everyone who listened was able to detect the slightest mistake the Skald might make. But such was the case.

For four hundred years the Skalds told their stories in verse. Their recitations took the place of our printed histories and geographies, our census records, our magazines, radios and popular songs.

Although much of this skaldic poetry is preserved, and the names of most of the very famous Skalds are known, the construction of the poems is so extremely complicated that it is practically impossible for us to enjoy them, even when they are carefully translated. The only foreigners who read skaldic poetry today are those whose business it is to study languages.

When we come to the Icelandic sagas, we find something quite different. The word saga means "something said," and our word "say" comes from it. The term is used to describe a great mass of stories, which were told from one generation to another for many years and which were finally written down.

The sagas are not in verse form, like skaldic poetry, but are in straightforward prose which is easy for Icelanders to read and easy to translate into other languages. They tell about people and places in Iceland and about kings and wars faraway. They tell about the pagan gods and goddesses and the seasons and storms and customs on earth and in heaven and under the earth.

Some of them are tremendously long. It is said that an Icelander came one summer to the court of Norway and the king was delighted with his ability to tell sagas. The king used to summon the visitor and command him to tell a story he had not told before. This went on for months until Christmas was approaching. The king called the saga teller into his presence and asked him if he had any sagas left. The Icelander said he had only one. The king ordered him to make it last as long as possible. So for twelve days the Icelander entertained the court with this saga. The king asked him where he had learned it, and he replied that every summer he used to attend the assembly at Thingvellir and listen to a famous saga teller. And in that way he learned the sagas and was able to recite them himself.

For many, many years there was no thought of writing down the sagas. They were always told like stories by men who were skillful at this. But by and by, in the beginning of the twelfth century, the sagas were slowly collected and written down on parchment. Some of the parchments contained not one saga as told by one man, but a series of shorter stories told by several different men. Sometimes these tales were changed a little as they were put down. But the best of them are clear and exciting and great fun to read. Every Icelander has read some of the sagas, and has become familiar with the characters and the places they describe.

Among the many sagas there are two which may particularly interest you. The first one, Njals Saga, is about two men who were dear friends.

Njal was a learned man of noble character and he was married to a woman named Bergthora. Bergthora was a brave and truthful woman, but she was extremely proud and could not bear it if she thought anyone was insulting her.

Njal's best friend was named Gunnar and if you want to know what kind of a man the Icelanders of that time admired most, here is the saga's description of him.

Gunnar was a man of great stature, strong and very able in all sports. He could wield the sword or use the bow with either hand as he liked. With the sword he could play so dexterously that one seemed to see three in the air at the same time. He was the best bowman, and could hit everything he aimed at. He could leap more than his own height fully armed, and equally far both backward and forward. He could swim like a seal, and there was no play in which anyone could compare with him, so that it was said that he never had an equal. He was beautiful in appearance, with a fair complexion. His nose was well formed, with the tip bent slightly upward. He had bright blue eyes, ruddy cheeks, and a rich growth of blonde hair which was very becoming. He was courteous in manners, manly, fearless, kind and faithful to his friends, but very critical in the selection of them.

Gunnar had traveled in foreign lands, and had won honors there. When he came back home he rode to the Althing with a beautiful scarlet cloak on his shoulders and a golden ring on his arm and a gilt helmet on his head. A superb sword hung at his side.

All his old friends came crowding out of their booths to greet him, for he was gay and merry and kind and everyone liked him. Among the familiar faces there was one he had not seen before. This was the face of Hallgerda, a tall, handsome young woman, clad in a red dress and red cloak, and with her golden hair so long and so thick that she could wrap it around herself like a mantle.

Hallgerda was a wicked woman who had already been married twice, and ruined both her husbands. But she was fascinating, and before Gunnar left the Althing he had asked her to marry him, and she had promised she would.

When Gunnar told Njal that he was going to marry Hallgerda, Njal was very sad. He told Gunnar that nothing but unhappiness could come from such a woman. But Gunnar did not believe him and said that no marriage and no woman could ever come between Njal and him and spoil their friendship.

Gunnar and Hallgerda were married and immediately Hallgerda began to make trouble. At a party at Njal's house, she insulted Bergthora, Njal's wife, and Bergthora was angry and answered back. The two husbands were troubled about this.

Once when Gunnar was returning from the Althing he brought a crowd of friends home with him. Hallgerda thought she needed some more food for all these people, and she forced one of her servants to go to a near-by farm and steal as much cheese and butter from the storehouse as he could load on two horses. Then he was to set fire to the place so that the owner would not discover the theft, but just think it was an accident and that the butter and cheese had been destroyed in the fire. The servant did not want to do this but Hallgerda threatened to have him killed if he refused and so he went, stole the provisions and set fire to the storehouse.

When Gunnar and all his guests came to the table, Gunnar asked Hallgerda where she had obtained so much cheese and butter. She retorted that it was not his business to trouble himself about her housekeeping. Then Gunnar became angry and said it certainly was his business, if it made him a sharer of stolen goods, and with that he gave her a slap on the cheek. Hallgerda vowed she would never forget that slap and she would repay it. You will see how she kept her word.

The quarrel between Hallgerda and Bergthora grew into a feud—which is a kind of war between two families or clans, and which may be continued from one generation to another. Gunnar and Njal tried to preserve their friendship, although their wives and relatives and servants were always fighting. Finally Gunnar's enemies decided to kill him. A number of them gathered together and surrounded his house. Gunnar had only his bow and arrows to protect himself and his household, but he was so skillful and strong that he was able to keep them off, wounding eight of them and slaying two others. But one of his enemies managed to cut his bow string with a sword. Gunnar then called to Hallgerda and asked her to cut off a lock of her long, thick hair and twist him a new bow string. But she reminded him of the slap he had once given her and refused to help him in any way. So Gunnar was unable to protect himself and was slain by his enemies.

Njal grieved for the friend he had known so long and loved so deeply and Njal's sons determined to revenge Gunnar's death. This prolonged the bitter feud and bloodshed. Finally, on a windy night, the enemies of Njal's sons gathered around Njal's house and told him they intended to burn it down with him and his sons inside. They said the women and children might come out unharmed, but no fighting man would be allowed to escape. Now Njal's wife, Bergthora, was a very different kind of woman from Hallgerda, who refused to help her husband when he was attacked. When the enemies called on her to come out of the house, she replied, "Young I was when I was given to Njal and we have promised that one fate shall befall us both."

Njal said, "We will go to our bed and lay us down. I have long been eager for rest."

Their little grandson was standing near and Bergthora took him and started to lead him outside. But the child refused, saying he would rather die with her and his grandfather than live without them.

So the old couple lay down on their bed, with the little boy between them. They made the sign of the cross and commended their souls to God. And those were the last words men heard them speak.

There is a great deal more to the saga than the stories of Gunnar and Njal, but this will give you some idea of it.

Another saga which is much loved by Icelanders is that of Grettir the Strong.

In order to understand this saga, you must know about outlaws. These were people who had broken some law and were condemned either to leave the country for a certain length of time, or, if they remained, to live by themselves, faraway from all other people. If they did not go abroad but preferred to stay in Iceland, they had to seek out some lonely spot to hide in. These outlaws would build a hut or live in a cave, stealing sheep for food.

Sometimes they raided farms or robbed travelers. There are stories about hidden valleys in the mountains where outlaws and their descendants lived for generations. Such valleys have occasionally been stumbled into by men who were searching for their stray sheep or had lost their way in a fog. These unexpected visitors were usually treated well by the outlaws, who led them back, often blind-folded, to the neighborhood of their homes.

Grettir the Strong, who lived more than a thousand years ago, was such an outlaw. He was, as his nickname implies, extremely powerful and daring. He was inclined to be silent and to keep more or less to himself. He could be gentle and merry or he could be rude and melancholy. He was kind and helpful to people in need, but when he became angry, he would kill a man. No one ever questioned his strength or his courage, and yet he had one strange weakness. He was afraid of the dark!

This saga about Grettir the Strong tells of his boyhood and the pranks he played and the verses he made up and the games he took part in.

He was still quite young when he had a quarrel with another man and killed him, and for this he was banished —or outlawed—to Norway for three years. While he was there, he got into trouble by again killing a man and for this he was outlawed from Norway, as he had been from Iceland.

The saga relates how he returned to Iceland and had all sorts of adventures, both with his friends and his enemies and even with ghosts. When he again killed a man and was again outlawed, he could not go back to Norway, but had to flee to some hideout in Iceland. For nineteen years he was persecuted and driven from place to place.

After about seventeen years of this lonely, hunted existence, he was at one time staying with his mother, who had hidden him from the sight of everyone. She wanted to keep him with her, but he was afraid that harm would come to her if he stayed. It was hard for him to leave her, for his fear of the dark had grown more and more, so that he was afraid to go anywhere after dusk. Finally the time came when he knew he must go away. His younger brother, Illugi, who loved him very much, went with him. Grettir was grateful for this. He said, "I can no longer live alone, even to save my life."

Off the northern coast of Iceland there is an island that looks like a great, square, bare castle rising from the water. This is the island of Drangey, and it was here that Grettir decided to live. He induced a kind man to row him out to it. With him went Illugi and a servant they had picked up on their journey. This man's name was Glaum, and he was a stupid, lazy and sulky fellow.

The sides of the island are so steep that no one can

climb them without a ladder, and Grettir knew that he
could pull up or knock down any ladder that was raised.
He and Illugi and Glaum lived there for two years, with
a pet gray ram called Gray Belly, with which they used
to frolic and play. They would climb down to the base
of the cliff-like walls and gather drift wood for the fire.
There were some sheep that had been brought over to
the island and left to graze, and they killed and ate one of
these when they wanted food, and they caught sea birds
and gathered their eggs.

The island was owned by about twenty men, and in
the spring they rowed out to it to get the sheep they had
left there to graze. They were surprised to see men on the
flat top of the cliffs, but took it for granted that they had
been shipwrecked and had climbed up the ladders to
safety. However, when they went to where the ladders
were, the men on top pulled the ladders up. The owners
of the island and Grettir shouted back and forth about
the sheep. The owners of the flock offered to take Grettir
back to shore and said he need not pay anything for the
sheep he had killed. But Grettir would not go back with
them, nor would he let them take away any of their animals. As he had control of the ladders, there was nothing
they could do except to go away.

That same spring Grettir began feeling restless and
thought he would like to go back to the mainland. Illugi

and Glaum begged him not to, but he went in spite of them. He put on a sort of disguise and went to the assembly or Thing at Hegranes. No one recognized him and they asked him to join in the wrestling games. When, singlehanded and alone, he defeated the two strongest men there at once, they knew he must be Grettir the Strong. However, they promised they would not harm him but let him go back to his island.

One night, after Grettir had been two years in Drangey, Glaum, whose duty it was to tend the fire, let it go out. Of course, no one had matches in those days and Grettir thought that the best way to start a new fire was to go back to the mainland and get some. As there was no boat passing, he decided to swim across to the shore, which was a mile away. He prepared for this by making himself some swimming clothes and fashioned a web between his fingers and he swam the distance without difficulty. He found the man who had first rowed him out to Drangey. He was willing to row him back and let him carry some fire with him. The fact that Grettir swam that long distance from the island to the mainland has made him even more famous.

According to the saga, one of the men who owned Drangey and had tried to get Grettir to leave it, had a foster mother who was a witch. Having failed to get

Grettir off the island by talks and threats, he now decided to ask his foster mother to cast a spell on him. The old woman had him take her to the water's edge, where she found a large stump of a tree which was lying on the shore. She had turned it over so it showed the smooth, flat underside. On this she cut some symbols, and reddened them with her blood. Then she had her foster son push the stump into the sea and it drifted toward Drangey. When Grettir found the stump, he was suspicious of it and prodded it back into the sea. The second day he found it again, this time nearer the ladder, and again he prodded it into the sea. But the third day, when Glaum was sent to get fuel, he brought the log up the ladder. Grettir did not notice what tree stump it was and started to chop it up. As soon as the axe touched the tree, it slid off and cut into Grettir's right leg.

At first he and Illugi thought the leg was healing perfectly, but soon they discovered it was swelling and turning blue. Nothing they could do seemed to help it.

While Grettir was lying there, weakened by his sickness, and Illugi was sitting beside him, they told Glaum to watch the ladder and keep away any enemies. But Glaum fell asleep and the enemies came, climbed the ladder and attacked Grettir. He and Illugi fought valiantly, but Grettir was finally killed and after him Illugi, who had defended him with such bravery and courage. Thus it was witchcraft in the end which brought Grettir to his death.

These sagas of Njal and Grettir are very long, for what you have read here is only a small part of them, but you can see that they are something like our stories of Robin Hood and Robinson Crusoe.

Besides the sagas there are many folk tales and fairy tales. There are stories about elves, giants, ghosts, sorcerers and outlaws and finally such stories as are called in Icelandic "dvintyri" from which comes our English word "adventure." The story of Hlini, the King's Son, which you will read in the next chapter, is a story of adventure. There are also tales of miracles and holy men.

The elves in Iceland are not like our fairies. They are called "the hidden people" and that word explains very clearly how the Icelanders think of them. They act just like other people, but are hidden from the eyes of men. They live in rocks and only once in a while may they be seen. This is most apt to happen on New Year's Eve, when they are moving from one rock to another. At that time they drive in sleds over the ice. The sleds are drawn by beautiful horses and the elf people wear their costliest clothes. They do not harm human beings, if they are well

treated and well spoken of. But if they are offended, they may find a way to revenge themselves.

The giants of Iceland live in caves in the mountains and sometimes kill lonely travelers or shepherd boys and eat them. They not only steal sheep, but many even steal the beautiful daughters of farmers. There are, however, some giants who are kind to human beings who have been kind to them. There are stories, too, about the "night giants." These wander around during the night and if

125

they have not reached their caves before the sun rises, they turn to stone.

In general, the ghost stories are very much the same as they are all over the world, but because the winter nights are so long and so dark, perhaps Icelandic ghost stories are particularly frightening.

Then there are stories of sorcerers, who were like our witches and were supposed to practice all sorts of secret and wicked arts.

In the next chapter you may read some of these stories and see for yourself what they are like.

# XII.    SOME ICELANDIC FAIRY TALES

*(Retold by Sigrídur Ingimarsdóttir)*

### *The Story of Hlini, the King's Son*

ONCE upon a time a king lived with his queen at their palace. They had one son named Hlini, and he was at that time one of the bravest and most promising young men in the whole country. Not far from there, a farmer lived with his wife in a small cottage. They had one daughter whose name was Signy.

One day the king's son went hunting with his father's courtiers. When they had caught several deer and birds, a thick fog fell upon them, so that the courtiers lost sight of Hlini. When they arrived back at the palace, they told the king that his son had disappeared and they could not find him anywhere. On hearing this, the king became very sad, and he sent out many people to look for Hlini. The search went on for three days, but the king's son was nowhere to be found. The king was so struck with grief that he did not rise from his bed, just as if he were ill. He now had an announcement made that whoever found his son would get half of his kingdom as a reward.

Signy, the farmer's daughter, heard of Hlini's disappearance and the reward the king had promised. She went to her parents and asked them to give her new shoes and some food, and then she started off. When she had walked nearly all day, she came to a cave. She entered the cave and there she saw two beds spread with beautiful coverlets—one woven with gold and the other with silver. All of a sudden she discovered that the lost prince lay in the bed with the golden coverlet, sound asleep. She tried to wake him up, but could not. Then she observed that some words were written on the beds, but she did not know their meaning. She therefore hid behind the door. Hardly had she found this hiding place when she heard a thundering noise outside and saw two huge giantesses enter the cave. One of them sniffed suspiciously and exclaimed, "Fi, our cave smells of men!" But the other one told her that the smell came from Hlini. Then they went over to his bed and said:

> "Sing, sing, my swans
> Until Hlini awakens"

And some swans just outside the cave sang and Hlini woke up. The younger of the two giantesses offered him something to eat but he refused. Then she asked him if he would have her for his wife, but he flatly refused. Then she shouted:

> "Sing, sing, my swans
> Until Hlini falls asleep."

The swans sang until he slept. Then the giantesses lay down on the other bed and fell asleep, too. The next morning they awakened Hlini as they had done before and again offered him food, but he did not accept anything from them. Once more, the younger giantess asked him if he would have her for his wife, but he refused as before. Then they put him to sleep again and left the cave.

Shortly after they had gone, Signy came from her hiding place and woke up the prince as the giantesses had done. He was very relieved to see her. She told him of his father's grief for him, and he explained to her how he had lost his way in the fog and met the two giantesses, who had taken him to this place and cast a spell on him so that he could not step out of the cave. As she had heard, one of them was trying to force him to take her for his wife, but he had steadfastly refused.

"Tonight, when she asks you this same question," Signy said, "you must promise her to accept the offer if she is willing to tell you what is written on these beds and furthermore what she and the other giantess are doing in the woods during the day."

The prince agreed to this. Then he took out a chess-board and asked Signy to play with him. They played until late in the afternoon, then the farmer's daughter put him to sleep and hid herself. Soon the giantesses rushed in, bringing with them a bunch of birds they had caught. They made a fire and the older one started cooking, but the younger one awakened Hlini and offered him food, which he accepted. When he had eaten, she asked him once more if he would have her for his wife. He told her he would do as she wished, if she were willing to tell him the meaning of the rhymes which were written on the beds. She told him that the inscription was:

Glide, my bed, glide
Anywhere I want to go.

"But tell me something more," Hlini said. "What are you two doing in the woods during the day?" She told him that they were hunting most of the time, and the rest of the time they would sit under a great oak, tossing their life-egg between them. He asked if this egg was of any value to them and she told him that they would both die if the egg were broken. The prince thanked her for telling him this, and asked her to put him to sleep again, so that he could rest during the night.

The next morning the younger giantess brought Hlini some food, which he accepted as before. Then she asked him if he did not want to go hunting with them in the woods. He told her that he preferred to remain in the cave and she put him to sleep, after which both of the giantesses left.

When the giantesses had gone, Signy awakened the prince and asked him to rise. "Now we must follow your captors to the woods," she said. "Take your spear with you and when they start playing with the life-egg, throw the spear at it. But your own life is at stake if you miss it."

The prince consented to this. Then they both sat on his bed and said:

"Glide, my bed, glide,
Glide to the woods."

And the bed took them to the woods and did not stop until they came to the great oak. There they heard the sound of roaring laughter. Signy told the prince to climb the oak and he did so. Peering down, he saw that the two giantesses were sitting under the tree. One of them had a golden egg in her hand, which she threw at the other. At this very instant the prince threw his spear at the egg, and hit it as it flew through the air. This so startled the giantesses that they fell foaming to the ground. The prince then climbed down from the oak and hurried with Signy to the cave, where they gathered up all the valuables they could find there and loaded both the beds with them. Then one of them sat on each bed and recited the magic words. The beds glided out of the cave and carried them and all the treasures to the farmer's cottage, where they received a warm welcome from the farmer and his wife, and spent the night with them.

Early the next morning Signy went to the palace, presented herself before the king and asked him what he would give her if she brought him back his son, safe and sound. The king said that he would hardly have to answer that question because she could not have succeeded in the search better than his clever, stalwart men. Signy then asked whether she would receive the reward he had promised if she could find his son. He agreed to that and Signy went back to the cottage and requested Hlini to come with her to the palace.

The king heartily welcomed his son, offered him the seat at his right hand and requested him to relate everything which had happened to him after he lost sight of his men. The prince sat down, seated Signy on his other side and told his father the whole story—how Signy had rescued him from the giantesses and saved his life. When the story was finished, Hlini rose to his feet and asked his father's consent to marry the farmer's daughter, which the king granted at once. He ordered a feast for the young couple and invited all the nobles of his kingdom.

The wedding celebrations lasted for a week and when they were over, everyone went to his home laden with gifts from the king and praising his generosity. Signy and Hlini lived happily ever after—and that is the end of this story.

## The Story of Gilitrutt

Once upon a time there lived a young farmer near the south coast of Iceland. He was a clever man and a good worker. There were fine pastures on his farm and he had many sheep. At the time of this story he was newly married. His wife was young, but sluggish and inactive. She was too lazy to work and did not care much about housekeeping. The farmer did not approve of this, but could, however, do nothing about it. One autumn he brought her quantities of wool from which he asked her to weave some cloth during the winter, but she paid hardly any attention to him.

The winter passed on and the farmer's wife did not touch the wool, even though her husband often reminded her of it. One day an old woman, very gigantic in appearance, came to her and asked her help. "Can you do something for me in turn?" the housewife asked.

"I could," answered the old hag, "but what do you want me to do?"

"Weave some cloth from my wool," the housewife told her.

"Give it to me," the other said. The woman gave her a great bag of wool, which she tossed on her back, declaring, "I'll bring you the cloth on the first day of summer."

"How much shall I pay you for it?"

"Nothing much. You only have to guess my name, but you must guess right the third time you try." The housewife agreed and the old hag left with the bag of wool.

The winter passed away, and the farmer often asked his wife where the wool was, but she told him not to bother his head about it, she would give him the cloth on the first day of summer.

As summer drew near, the housewife started thinking

about the old woman's name, but did not know how to find it out. This caused her great anxiety. The farmer saw that something ailed her and asked her to tell him what it was. Finally, she told him the whole story. The farmer became very frightened, for he knew that the old woman must have been a giantess, who probably intended to rob him of his wife.

Some days later, when the farmer was walking in the mountains near his farm, he came upon a rocky hill. He was thinking about his ill fortune and hardly knew where he went. All of a sudden he heard a noise from inside the hill. He moved quietly in the direction of the sound and found a small gap between the rocks. He peeped through and saw a gigantic woman sitting at a loom weaving. As she wove she sang:

"Hi, hi, ho, ho, the housewife does not know my name, but Gilitrutt it is, hi, hi, ho, ho."

She sang this over and over again and wove on. The farmer brightened up, for he presumed that this was the woman who had called on his wife last autumn. He went home and wrote down the name Gilitrutt on a piece of paper, but did not tell his wife of his discovery.

On the last day of winter, the housewife was so overcome with worry that she did not rise from her bed. Her husband then came to her and asked her if she knew the weaver's name. She shook her head and informed him that she was going to lie in bed and grieve herself to death. He told her that this would not be necessary, gave her the piece of paper and related to her the whole story of the giantess in the cave. She took the paper with trembling hands, for she feared that the name was wrong. She asked her husband to stay with her when the woman came.

"No," he told her, "you did not ask my advice when you gave her the wool, so now you must pay her without any help from me."

The first day of summer came and the farmer's wife lay in bed, alone in the house. Then the old woman entered with a thundering noise. She was anything but pleasant to look at. She threw a big bundle of homespun cloth on the floor and said, "Now, what's my name, what's my name?"

The housewife, who was more dead than alive from fear, said weakly, "Signy, that's my name, that's my name."

The old hag laughed. "Guess again, housewife."

"Asa, that's my name, that's my name."

"Guess once more, housewife."

"It would not be Gilitrutt?" the woman asked.

This so surprised the hag that she fell to the floor with a boom. Then she rose to her feet, went away and was never seen after that.

The farmer's wife was exceedingly relieved at having got rid of this monster and rapidly changed for the better. From that day on, she was as diligent as she had been lazy before, cheerfully minded her housekeeping and worked on her wool unaided.

### The Elves and Helga, the Farmer's Daughter

Once there lived a farmer with his wife in the southern part of Iceland. They had two daughters and thought much of the older one, but the younger, whose name was Helga, they neglected.

In those days it was the custom for all who could to go to church on Christmas Eve, except the one who was left at home to mind the cattle and look after the house. Now at this particular farm the watchmen had for several years been found dead when the people came back home from church on Christmas morning. This went so far that finally no one wanted to keep watch on that night.

One Christmas Eve, when all the people on the farm left for church as usual, Helga was ordered by her parents to stay at home and milk the cows, look after the animals and cook the smoked meat for the Christmas dinner. Her parents thought there would be little harm in losing her anyhow and said so. Then all the people started off.

Helga fed the livestock first. Then she swept the

house thoroughly and started cooking the meat. When it was nearly done, a little boy entered the kitchen, carrying a small wooden vessel in his hand. The child greeted Helga, and she answered him kindly. He asked her to put a wee bit of meat and some gravy in the bowl which he handed to her. Helga did so, even though her mother, before she left, had harshly warned her not to eat or give away any of the meat or gravy. When the vessel had been filled, the child thanked Helga and trotted away.

When Helga had finished her work, she lit a lamp in the living room, took off her shoes, sat on her parents' bed and started reading. After a while she heard a great noise and the sound of voices outside, and soon she observed that the house was full of people who crowded into the living room, so that she could hardly move. These newcomers started amusing themselves with dancing and singing, but paid no attention to Helga and she did not interfere with them either.

Later in the evening, when she intended to go out and milk the cows, she found that the room was so crowded that she could not even turn around. One of the guests, an elderly man with a long beard, who was much taller than the rest, called out and asked the people to make room for Helga so that she could get at her shoes and make her way around the house. The people did so and Helga went out into the darkness, leaving the lamp burning for the visitors. She had just started milking when she heard someone enter the stable. This person greeted her and she responded kindly. The stranger, who was a man, asked if she would allow him to kiss her. She refused. He asked her this same question several times, but she always refused. Then he left her.

A little later the stable was entered again, this time by a woman, who also greeted Helga. This woman thanked Helga warmly for the kindness she had shown her child and for having refused her husband's request just before. Having said this, she gave Helga a bundle, which she asked her to accept as a reward for this service. "In this parcel," she said, "you will find clothes fit for you to wear on your wedding day and also a belt, which you will not have to be ashamed of then. You shall be a fortunate woman and marry a bishop. Never give the clothes away and do not wear them until your wedding day."

Helga took the parcel and thanked the visitor for her present. Then the elf-woman departed.

When Helga had finished the milking, she went back to the house. The people made room for her as before. She again sat on the bed and continued her reading. Towards dawn, the people started leaving, one by one, and by daybreak they had all departed.

When Helga was all alone, she opened the parcel and found that the elf-woman had given her the most beautiful clothes she had ever seen but the belt was the most exquisite of all. She put the parcel away in a safe place.

When the household came back from church on Christmas morning, Helga had fed the cattle and finished the housework.

"She is unharmed, of course, even though no one would have missed her had she passed away," her parents said when they saw that Helga was safe and sound.

They could not get much out of her about the happenings of the night. However, she showed them the lovely clothes the elf-woman had given her. They greatly admired them, especially the belt. Her mother and sister tried to get the clothes for themselves, claiming that Helga was not fit to wear them, so she took them away and locked them up in her chest.

The next Christmas Eve, Helga's mother and sister decided to stay at home to see if the elf-woman would not also bring them gifts. In the end, however, the farmer's wife alone remained at home when the others left for church. Nothing is known of the woman's doings, except that when she was cooking the meat for Christmas a child entered the room, carrying its small wooden vessel. The child greeted the woman and asked her to put a wee bit of meat and some gravy into the vessel. The woman grew angry and refused to give it anything.

"Your people may be much richer than I am," she declared.

The child repeated its pleas and this enraged the woman so much that she struck the vessel out of the child's hand so hard she broke its arm. The child started crying, picked up the vessel with its whole arm and ran away, howling loudly. No one knows what happened to the woman after that, but when the members of the household came back from church, they found her lying on the floor with her bones broken and covered with blood. She could only with great effort tell the people of the child and how she had treated it, then she died. Everything in the house had been broken and torn apart and all the food there was had been spoiled, too. But from that day on nothing like this ever happened at the farm on Christmas Eve.

Helga stayed with her father a few years after her mother's death, then she went to Skalholt—then one of the two Lutheran episcopal seats in Iceland—and there she married the bishop, as the elf-woman had predicted. On her wedding day she wore the beautiful dress and handsome belt and was admired by everyone. After that she lived a long and happy life—and that ends this story.

GEORGE
GRAY
ICELAND

## The Origin of the Elves

In Iceland, this story is told about the origin of the
elves. Once God called on Adam and Eve. They welcomed him heartily and showed him everything they had,
including their children, of whom He was very fond.
He asked Eve, if she did not have more children than the
ones she had shown him. She denied this. But the truth
was that she had not had time to wash all her children
before God arrived and hid some of them, because she
was ashamed of letting Him see them unwashed. But
God, Who knows everything, also knew that she was
lying, and He said, "What is hidden from Me, shall also
be hidden from men." The unwashed children then be-

came invisible to the eyes of men and lived in the hills and rocks, and from them the elves descended. But the children Eve showed to God are the forefathers of men. Moreover, men never can see the elves, unless they want to be seen, but the elves can see men and appear to them when they like.

## XIII.   PIRATES, A PASTOR AND SOME POEMS

A LONG time ago Iceland had a hard time with pirates. To be sure, there were pirates everywhere then—even up and down the coast of the United States. And to be sure, the inhabitants of Iceland had been guilty of some piracy, too, when they sailed down to Ireland and captured men and women and brought them back to work as slaves.

But in any case, the pirates seem to have been especially

fierce when they made their raids on Iceland, and this seems strange, for the island was not only faraway for sailing vessels and rowboats to reach, but it was also very poor in the kind of treasure pirates usually want.

It all began in 1579, when a boatload of English pirates appeared without any warning and swarmed up the coast in the Vestfjords. The Icelanders were taken by surprise and furthermore they were helpless, for they were under Danish rule and forbidden to carry or even to own weapons. The pirates robbed the churches, killed the men who tried to defend themselves and their families, and seized the governor and held him for a large ransom. They forbade him to report this to the King of Denmark, but the governor did manage to send word about the raid, and the King of Denmark had the pirates hunted down, caught and executed.

This, however, did not keep other pirates from sailing up to Iceland, coming ashore and stealing and murdering. Spanish pirates came (in 1614) and took away all the sheep and cattle they could and whatever else the farmers and fishermen had. English pirates came to the Westman Islands. They were led by a man whose name does not describe him very well, for that name was John Gentlemen. This particular gang did not kill anyone, but they frightened people by screaming and howling and by pointing their muskets at them and threatening them and then laughing at and making fun of them. They took the church bell out of the little church and fastened it on their mast and sailed away.

There were lots of other raids, and finally things became so dangerous that King Christian IV of Denmark —who was also King of Iceland—sent out some war vessels to drive the pirates off the sea.

The war vessels were not very successful, for the worst raid of all happened after that, in 1627. This was on the Westman Isles, which were frequently chosen for raids because they were so faraway from the mainland that other Icelanders could not get there quickly to help their kinsfolk and friends.

Well, a big gang of Algerian pirates suddenly appeared off the coast in three ships, with a hundred men in each ship. They sailed right into the main harbor and rushed up on the shore, for the inhabitants of the islands were without weapons and powerless to stop them. Shouting and yelling and brandishing cutlasses, they swarmed over the whole island, killing anyone who tried to get away or to protect himself. After they had driven practically everyone left alive into a large storehouse, they chose the youngest and strongest of the islanders and drove these aboard their ships. Then they set fire to the building and burned to death those who were inside. There was a Lutheran pastor there, kneeling in prayer, and the Alge-

rians struck him dead and took his wife and children
away with them.

They sailed back to Algeria with whatever they had
stolen and sold the three or four hundred men and women
and children they had captured as slaves. Most of them
died, and those who managed to live wrote such sad
letters back to Iceland that the Icelanders and the Danes
collected enough money to buy their liberty. After ten
years, only thirty-eight of the original three or four
hundred captives were now alive. Among them was a
woman whose story you may now read.

Her name was Gudridur Simonardsdottir, and she had
been married and was living in the Westman Isles at the
time of the raid. The pirates took her with them and sold
her with seventeen other women as slaves in Algeria. She
was probably the most attractive of them all, for the son
of the Governor of Algiers wanted to marry her. When
the ransom money was sent by Denmark, more was demanded for her than for anyone else. This ransom money
was equal to the value of 393 sheep.

Now since these Icelanders had been held captive in
Algeria for ten years, those who were children when
they were captured had grown up not knowing how to
speak Icelandic or Danish. Furthermore, all of the captives had been forced to give up the Christian religion
and become Mohammedans, for that was the religion of

their conquerors and masters.

These captives, whose liberty had been purchased, were now taken to Copenhagen, in Denmark, on their way back to Iceland. A tutor was found there to teach the children not only their native language, but also the Christian religion, which the children had never known and which the grown people had almost forgotten. The tutor who was chosen was an Icelander living in Copenhagen whose name was Hallgrimur Petursson.

Hallgrimur had had a hard life. He had been born in Iceland and was being educated there, when he decided to leave home and go to Denmark. We do not know just what made him do this, but we do know that when he was sixteen he was working as an apprentice to a black-smith in Copenhagen.

The blacksmith treated him cruelly and Hallgrimur ran away from the shop. On the street he met a distant cousin of his who arranged for him to go to college in Copenhagen.

This was his second chance to get an education, and this time he made the most of it. He had been at school for four years and was doing well when the thirty-eight liberated Icelanders arrived from Algeria, and Hall-grimur was appointed as their tutor.

He was twenty-two at this time and Gudridur was thirty-eight or sixteen years older than he. But that did not make any difference. They fell in love and in the spring Hallgrimur determined to go back to Iceland with Gudridur and the other Icelanders who had been captured and were now ransomed.

Gudridur had been married at the time of the Algerian raid, and she did not know whether her husband was alive now or not. When she and Hallgrimur reached Iceland, they made sure her husband was dead and then they were married. There were many things about this marriage which people did not approve of. The sweethearts had not waited to find out about Gudridur's husband before they acted as if they were man and wife, and they had a child before they were married. Furthermore, Gudridur had grown to like and believe certain things in the Mohammedan religion and this was a grief to Hallgrimur, since he wanted to become a Lutheran pastor. At first he and his wife were dreadfully poor and he hired himself out as a day laborer to any merchant or farmer who would have him.

Finally, truly repenting his past, he did manage to become a Lutheran pastor, but his troubles were by no means over.

His congregation did not like him. They did not approve of the way he had come back to Iceland from Denmark with a woman who was so much older than he, who had been a slave and was inclined to believe in Mohammedanism. They showed their dislike by playing all sorts of mean practical jokes on Hallgrimur. Once he was accused of spilling the wine on the floor during the Communion Service. This was a very serious offense. It was not until later that he found out that one of his enemies had bored a hole in the bottom of the chalice before the services commenced. They hid the Altar Book in a filthy cow stall and laughed when he had to hunt for it. In fact, for seven years they teased and tormented him and Gudridur. He accepted it all meekly and continued his preaching and wrote Biblical poems, until finally he became known as a kind and faithful pastor and also as a gifted writer.

After seven difficult years, he was moved to another parish and here he was happier. He had a little more money now, his congregation liked him and his poems were becoming more widely known.

To understand how he came to write these poems, you will have to remember that at this time very few people could read. Hallgrimur was an earnest Christian and he wanted the farmers and fishermen and their wives and children to know the Bible. He tried to think of some way it could be taught to them so they would remember and understand it.

As you read in the last chapter, the Icelanders have always been extremely fond of poetry. They have liked

to hear historical stories told in verse and enjoyed recit-
ing them or listening to other people recite them.

Hallgrimur thought if he could put some of the Bible
stories into verse, people would like hearing them and
they would remember them more easily. So for a number
of years he selected various parts of the Bible and put
them into verse form. These verses served a double purpose. People not only learned them easily but they liked
to sing them as hymns. Before this, the only hymns they
had were translations from Danish, German or Latin.

Hallgrimur's versification of the Bible was not a great
piece of art. He was not trying to write splendid poetry,
but merely to teach the Bible in such a way people could
remember it. But he learned a great deal about rhyme and
rhythm and meter, so that when the time came for him
to write his great poetry he knew all about the form.

He wrote many things besides the verses and hymns.
He wrote several books and booklets on religious subjects
and became well known throughout Iceland. His house
at Sourby burned down. He lost everything he owned
and wrote one of his most beautiful hymns about his grief
over this loss.

Although Hallgrimur had always been poor, he had
not complained about that. He had suffered from bad
treatment for seven years in his first parish and he had
accepted it without thought of revenge. But when he

was fifty years old an affliction much more terrible than any of these befell him.

He was stricken with leprosy.

Iceland is one of the healthiest places in the world today and there have been no new cases of leprosy for many, many years. But at that time it was a fairly common disease and Hallgrimur suffered from it for the last ten years of his life. During this time he wrote his Passion Hymns, which are more loved in Iceland than any other poetry.

There are fifty of these, and they tell the whole story of Christ's last days on earth, from the Garden of Gethsemane to Golgotha. They are written with such beauty and sincerity and emotion and wisdom that they became popular immediately. Furthermore, they have remained so all these years since Hallgrimur's death in 1674. They have been translated into many languages, but it is difficult to translate Icelandic poetry, and so, unless you can read Icelandic, you cannot really know how beautiful these hymns are, and why they mean so much to Iceland.

The years when Hallgrimur was alive were practically the most miserable and wretched in the whole history of Iceland. People were poor and sick and discouraged. Volcanic eruptions had ruined their farms. Denmark taxed them heavily. As we read about these times, it seems a miracle that the Icelanders had any ambition or courage

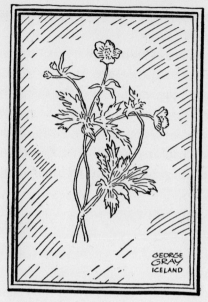

to continue to live and struggle.

And then Hallgrimur wrote his hymns, bringing hope to their hearts once more. He himself had known what it was to be poor and despised and tormented. He was suffering from a loathsome disease. And yet he was able to write so sweetly and with such faith in goodness that he encouraged the whole nation. People took heart and determined to do the best they could.

Hallgrimur is now so honored in Iceland that in 1914, on the three hundredth anniversary of his death, the whole nation celebrated the occasion. What will be, when it is completed, the largest church in Iceland is named for him.

As you read history you will notice how often it happens that just when times are darkest, some remarkable man or woman appears and saves the day. This was what happened in Iceland, when Hallgrimur wrote his Passion poems and saved his countrymen from despair.

In the next chapter you will read about two other men who changed their native land by their intelligence and bravery.

GEORGE
GRAY
ICELAND

## XIV.  A GREAT MAN AND A GREAT BOOK

IF you should motor from Reykjavik to Reyholt, you would see there a great, fine, modern boarding school. You would see a greenhouse heated by natural hot water and, if you went in summertime, you would see acres and acres of green grass blowing in the wind or hay turning golden in the sun.

But probably the thing which would interest you most would be in the rear of the school—an open air bathtub, into which is led the water from a near-by hot spring. It is circular and paved with stones and there is a covered passageway between it and the house. Of course, the house that was there seven hundred years ago has disappeared, but the bath and the passageway are just as they were when the man who lived at Reyholt used to recline in the hot water and talk about politics and poetry to his friends. Today many visitors throw a piece of money in the bathtub for good luck.

This man was named Snorri Sturlason and during his life he was the richest man in Iceland, the most powerful politician and the most distinguished scholar and writer. His riches no longer exist, and his politics are no longer argued, but the books he wrote are still read. One of these is fascinating, not only to Icelanders, but to almost anyone else. This is called *The Lives of Norse Kings.*

Snorri had spent a great deal of time in Norway and knew the country and its kings. He had also studied the history of long ago—not only the history of the Scandinavian countries, but of England and Ireland, Germany, France and Russia, and sometimes he found out and recorded events which had never been recorded before. Because he was extremely careful to be accurate, his books are valuable. Because he wrote so well, they are delightful to read.

Perhaps the best way for you to get an idea about this

particular book is to hear a few of the stories which are in it.

You remember that all Scandinavia was once pagan, and worshipped the pagan gods and goddesses. One of the kings of Norway was Olav Trygvason, and when he became converted to Christianity, he immediately went to work to convert everyone else. One time he went to a pagan temple and saw a row of statues of the heathen gods. Thor, who was the most honored, was decorated with gold and silver. Olav knocked his statue down with his spiked axe. Then all his followers knocked down the rest of the images of gods. When the king came out of the temple, he told the people who had gathered there that they must either accept Christianity or battle with him. They decided they would rather accept Christianity and so every single one was immediately baptized.

But although the King was such a violent Christian, he could not quite forget some of the old heathen gods. Once, when he was at a feast, there came to him a wise old man who wore a broad-brimmed hat and had only one eye. He had traveled in many lands and the king talked with him for a long time and found he could answer all questions. They sat and chatted so long that finally the bishop reminded the king that it was time to go to bed. So the king undressed and got into bed and the old man with one eye came and sat on the foot of the bed and they went on talking.

Finally the bishop said the king must now go to sleep, and the visitor went out. A little later, the king woke up and asked for the visitor, but no one could find him. The next morning, the king called to him his cook and his butler and asked them whether they had seen a stranger. They said that while they were preparing the meat for the next meal, a strange man with one eye had come to them and had given them two fat pieces of meat and told them to cook these with what they had. When the king heard this, he commanded his servants to throw away all the meat, since he felt that the stranger must be the pagan god, Odin, who was trying to bewitch him, for Odin had only one eye and he knew everything because he had two black ravens who flew through the world all day and returned at night to tell him what they had seen.

This book about the Norse kings has love stories in it, as well as stories about the pagan gods. One of the prettiest of these love stories is told of this same King Olav.

King Olav was the greatest man in all those kinds of sports that are told about in Norway. He was stronger and nimbler than any man, and there are many tales written about this. One relates how he went up the Smalsarhorn and fastened his shield on the top, and another tells of how he helped a guardsman of his who had climbed to the top and found that he could get neither up nor down; but the king went up to him and bore him down on his arm. King Olav also ran along the oars outside the ship when his men were rowing in the "Serpent," and he played with three hand swords, so that one was always up in the air and he always had hold of another by the hilt. He smote equally well with both hands and shot two spears at one time. King Olav was the gladdest of all men and very playful, blithe and forgiving, very heated in all things, generous and prominent amongst his fellows, bold before all in battle, but very gruesome when he was wroth and his foes he tormented much. Some he burned, some he let wild hounds tear asunder, and others he maimed or cast down from high mountains. Because of all these things, his friends loved him, but his foes were afraid of him; his success was great because some did his will out of love and friendship, but others out of fear.

When he was in England after the death of his first wife, he heard of a queen called Gyda. Gyda was a young and beautiful widow. She was very rich and powerful and she called for an assembly or Thing so that she could choose a husband for herself.

Olav went to the Thing under a false name and disguised himself by wearing his worst clothes. Gyda went and looked over every man who seemed to her to be manly. And when she came to where Olav stood, she asked, "Wilt thou have me? So I will choose thee."

"I will not say nay to that," he replied.

Olav then wed Gyda and stayed in England and Ireland for a while before he went back to Norway.

Then there is a story about the Danish King Harald Gormson. It had been made a law in Iceland that every man must compose an insulting verse about the king. This was because an Icelandic ship had been stranded off the coast of Denmark, and the Danes had taken everything it contained and reported that the boat had been wrecked.

King Harald sent a man to Iceland to find out how things were going there. Now this envoy was a trollman, which meant he was able to change his shape. This time he changed himself into a whale. When he reached Iceland, he saw land sprites flying about everywhere. He arrived at a fjord and a great dragon came down the valley, followed by serpents and toads and they blew poison at him. Then he went to another fjord, and a bird flew toward him so enormous that its wings touched the hills on each side of the fjord, and with it were many other birds both large and small. He then tried another fjord and a great ox came wading out toward him, bellowing horribly. So away went the whale to seek still another fjord, but he was met by a giant who had an iron staff in his hand and whose head was higher than the mountains and there were other giants with him.

Then the troll-man returned to Denmark and reported these things to King Harald, who decided not to go to Iceland, after all.

There is another story about King Eystein of Norway. He asked the people of a certain district in Norway if they would have as their king a slave of his called Tore the Hairy, or whether they would rather have his dog, who was named Saur. They chose the dog, for they thought that he would interfere with them least. Then they bewitched the dog so that he barked two words, but spoke every third word. They made a collar and a leash of gold and silver for him and when it was muddy, the king's guardsmen carried him on their shoulders. He had a highseat or throne on which he sat. But by and by the guardsmen grew tired of having a dog for a master and when the wolves came down on a sheepfold, they urged him to go forth and protect the sheep. The dog-king might have a golden collar, but he was a dog at heart and not a king. He attacked the wolves and was killed by them.

Such stories at these Snorri told, not because he believed they were true, but because the kings about whom he wrote thought they were true.

When Snorri wrote about actual battles and wars he was always exact. For instance, he tells how another Norse king who was also named Olav broke down London Bridge. This King Olav (who was later declared a saint and called St. Olav) was in England fighting. He and his men rowed their boats up under the bridge and put ropes around the wooden piles which supported it. Then the oarsmen rowed down stream with all their might. The piles were loosened, the bridge broke down and the armed forces standing on it fell into the water and many were killed. Perhaps the old nursery game, "London Bridge Is Falling Down," is based on this event.

There is another story about this King Olav and his younger brothers which goes like this:

It is said that when King Olav was at the feast with Asta, his mother, she led forth her children to show him. The king set his brother Guthorm on his knee, and on the other knee he set his brother Halvdan. The king looked on the boys, then he frowned and gazed wrathfully at them; the boys were afraid. Then Asta brought to Olav her youngest son, who was called Harald and who was three years old. The king frowned at him, but the boy looked straight back at him. Then the king took the boy by the hair and pulled it, but the boy took the king by the beard and tugged it. Then said the king: "Vindictive wilt thou be later on, my kinsman."

The day after, the king went out in the village with Asta his mother. They went to a tarn where Guthorm and Halvdan, Asta's sons, were playing. The boys had made great farms and great lathes or barns, with many cows and many sheep; for that was their game. A short way along the tarn there was a muddy creek, and there was Harald, and he had chips of wood which were floating in great numbers near the shore. The king asked him what that was for. They were, the little boy said, his war-ships. The king laughed at this and said: "It may be, my kinsman, that thou wilt sometime command ships."

Then the king called Halvdan and Guthorm to him, and he asked Guthorm: "What wouldst thou have most of, my kinsman?"

"Fields," the boy answered.

The king asked, "How great fields wouldst thou have?" Guthorm answered, "I would that all this ness that reaches out into the water were sown every summer."

At that time there were ten farms on it, so the king answered: "Much corn might grow thereon." Then the king asked Halvdan what he would have most of.

"Cows," he answered.

The king asked him: "How many cows wouldst thou have?"

Halvdan said: "So many that when they go to the water they stand as thickly as possible round the water."

The king declared: "Great possessions wilt thou have. That is like thy father."

Then the king asked Harald: "What wouldst thou have most of?"

"Huscarls (house servants)," he answered.

The king said: "How many wilt thou have?"

"I would like so many that at one meal they would eat my brother Halvdan's cows."

The king laughed at that and said to Asta, "Here, Mother, thou art certainly bringing up a king."

Nothing more is told of them at that time.

After King Olav died and was buried, rumors began to go around that there were miracles happening, because of his holiness.

The bishop heard these rumors and decided to see for himself whether they were true. The king had been buried for a little more than a year and the bishop ordered that the coffin be lifted out of the earth and unlocked. As soon as this was done, a fragrance filled the air, and when the bishop uncovered King Olaf's face, he was as rosy and handsome as if he were still alive. The only change was that his hair and beard had grown long. The bishop took a pair of scissors and cut off some of the hair and some of the beard. Then he had fire brought to him in a censer. He made the sign of the cross and put some incense and the hair in the fire. When the incense was all burned up, there lay the hair unburned, so the bishop declared that King Olav was truly holy and a saint.

Where his body had been buried, a spring of water bubbled up, and people who used this water were healed of their sicknesses. Afterwards, a church was built over the spring and the altar was set where the body had been buried. The miracles went on for a long time. Blind people who came to worship at the church regained their sight and a man who was dumb regained his voice.

Once St. Olav's shrine was being carried in a procession through the streets. Suddenly it grew so heavy that the men who were carrying it could not hold it up any more. They set it down and then they dug in the street beneath it. Here they found the body of a little child who had been murdered and hidden there. The body was taken away and properly buried, and the street mended. And then the men found they could lift the shrine and carry it easily, as they had been able to do before.

There is one story about two kings who were brothers, which you will enjoy reading just as Snorri wrote it. King

Eystein and King Sigurd were both staying at a certain place one winter, and one day King Eystein proposed that they play a game of matching their wits. King Sigurd would not answer when he heard this proposition.

"I see," said King Eystein, "that I must first start this game; I will take thee, my Brother, as a match for me. I do this because we have both an equal name and like possessions and I can make no difference between our kindred and breeding."

Then answered King Sigurd: "Dost thou not remember that I used to throw thee on thy back when I would and thou wast a year older, too?"

Then said King Eystein: "I remember no less that thou didst not win a game which demanded cleverness."

Then said King Sigurd: "Dost thou remember how it went with us when we swam? I could duck thee when I wanted."

King Eystein said: "I swam as far as thou and I could dive and swim under the water as well as thou; I could also go on ice skates and I knew no one who could beat me therein; thou couldst do it no better than an ox."

King Sigurd said: "There does not seem to be a more lordly and useful sport than to shoot well with a bow; I think that thou canst not stretch my bow, even if thou didst try it with thy feet."

Eystein answered: "I am not so strong with a bow as

thou, but there is less difference in our ability to shoot at a mark; but I can go much better on skis, and this, too, has been called a good sport before now."

King Sigurd said: "This, I think, is much more lordly; that he who is leader shall be a great man in the army, strong and more skillful with weapons than other men and easy to see and recognize when many are together."

King Eystein said: "It is no less outstanding for a man to be handsome, for the best ornament is allied to beauty; I can also make better laws than thou; likewise in whatsoever we talk of, I am much better spoken."

King Sigurd said: "It may be that thou hast learned more law tricks, for I have had much else to do, and no one denies that thou hast a smooth tongue; but many say that thou dost not keep thy word, that thou layest little weight on what thou dost promise and that thou speakest in order to please those who are with thee, and that is not kingly."

King Eystein said: "This happens when men bring their matters before me and I have to give the best advice to each man's case; thereafter another comes who has a case against the first and then it is necessary to even out differences so that both shall be at peace. It may happen that I then promise what I am asked for, because I wish all men to go happily from their meeting with me. It would be an easy matter for me to do as thou dost, to promise all men evil. I hear no man complaining that thou hast not fulfilled thy promises."

King Sigurd said: "It has been the talk of many men that the journey which I made from this land was very lordly but thou, meanwhile, didst sit at home like thy father's daughter."

King Eystein answered: "Now thou hast touched the boil! I would not have started this talk if I could not have answered thee about this; it seems as if I sent thee from home like my sister when thou wast ready for the journey."

King Sigurd said: "Thou must have heard that I held many battles in Serkland, and in them all I gained the victory and many kinds of costly booty, the like of which has never come to this land. I was thought most worthy there where I found the noblest men, but I believe that thou still lovest the home fires best."

"I went to Palestine," King Sigurd said, "and visited Apulia on the way, but did not see thee there, my brother. I gave Jarl Roger the Mighty the title of 'king' and had the victory in eight battles, and thou wast not present in any of them. Afterwards I traveled to our Lord's grave, and did not see thee there. On this voyage I came as far as the Jordon, where our Lord was baptized, and swam across the river; there I did not see thee either. On the other side of the river are some willow bushes. I tied a few of them into a knot and vowed that thou shouldst untie it. It is still waiting for thee down there and thou art called upon to fulfill this vow of mine."

Then King Eystein said: "There is not much that I can speak of compared to what thou hast achieved. I have heard that thou hast won many battles in foreign lands, but it might have been more useful for the land what I meantime did at home. North at Vagar I built booths for the fishing folks, so that poor people could get help, and earn their living. There I founded a priest's garden and endowed the church. Before this the place was almost heathen. These men will remember that Eystein was King of Norway. The road from Trondheim went once over Dovre-fell, where people were lost in bad weather or had to sleep out of doors and suffer hardships. There I built a mountain inn and gave it an income; those people will know that Eystein has been King of Norway. At Agdenes there is a dangerous rocky coast and no harbor; and many ships were lost every year. There is now a harbor and a landing place for wintering ships, also a church. Afterwards I raised beacons on the high fells and this I hope will be useful for the country. I built at Bergen a king's hall and the church of the Apostles, with an underground passage between the two. The kings that come after me will remember my name for that.

"I built St. Michael's Church and a monastery besides. I have also, my brother, shaped the laws so that the
people can now obtain justice, and when the laws are
kept the country will be better ruled. I have set a warp-
ing pole with iron rings in Sinholm sound. The Jämt-
land people are again under the Norse king's rule, and
this was brought about by blithe words and wise per-
suasion and not by force or fighting. Now these matters
are of small importance, still I do not know, if the people in the land are not better served by them, than if
thou hast killed black men in Serkland and sent them to
hell. When thou praisest thyself for good deeds, I think
these places I have built for chaste people will sooner
give peace to my soul. The knot thou hast tied for me,
I will not untie; but if I wished it, I could have tied such
a knot for thee that thou wouldst never have become
King of Norway. That could have been done when
thou camest back to Norway with only one ship and
camest alongside my powerful fleet. Let now wise men
say in what way thou art above me, and ye braggarts
shall know that there are still people in Norway who
are thine equals."

From these various selections you will see that Snorri's
*Lives of the Norse Kings* has many things in it besides
accounts of battles and wars.

Sometimes there are stories which are told just to make

us laugh. This one about the ugly foot is a direct translation from Snorri's own writing.

There was a man called Toraren Nevjolvson. He was an Icelander and his kin were from the Northland. He was not of great family, but he was wise and clever of speech, and bold in talk with princes. He was a great traveler and was abroad for long stretches of time. Toraren was an ugly man, and especially so because he was ill-shaped in the limbs. He had great, ugly hands, but his feet were very much uglier. Toraren was present in Tunsberg when these things happened which have been told of before. He was acquainted with King Olav. Toraren made ready the merchant ship he owned and would go to Iceland in the summer. King Olav had Toraren as a guest for some days and talked much with him. Toraren slept in the king's room. Early one morning the king lay awake, but the other men in the room were asleep; the sun had just risen, and there was much light within. The king said to Toraren: "I have been awake some time and I have seen a sight which seems of great worth; it is a man's foot, so ugly that I believe there will not be one uglier in the whole town," and he bade the others look and see whether it seemed the same to them. And all who saw it said truly that it was so.

Toraren understood then what they were talking about and answered: "There are few things so odd that you cannot expect to find the like to them, and it is most likely that it is so now."

The king said: "I will not hold with it that you can find so ugly a foot, even if I should bet on it."

Then Toraren answered: "I am ready to bet you that here in this house I can find an uglier foot."

The king said: "Then shall the one of us who is right crave a boon of the other."

"So shall it be," said Toraren: he stuck forth from the bedclothes the other foot, and it was no whit fairer and the big toe was off, too. Then said Toraren: "Look here, O king, at another foot, which is so much uglier, as there is a toe off. I have won the bet."

The king said: "The first foot is so much uglier as there are five ugly toes on it, but on this only four. I have the right to crave a boon of thee."

So the king won the bet, after all.

During his lifetime Snorri was recognized as the most powerful man in Iceland, but he was not loved. Some Icelanders felt he was disloyal to Iceland and was trying to bring her under Norwegian power. On the other hand, the King of Norway thought he was disloyal to Norway. In fact, he was so angry with him he sent word to his agent in Iceland—a man named Gissur—to send Snorri back to Norway or to kill him.

*Arms of Iceland when a Kingdom*

Gissur came to Reyholt with seventy men, and broke into the house while Snorri was asleep and they killed him.

Today the Icelanders have forgotten Snorri's faults and they think of him as the greatest writer and scholar Iceland has ever had. Norway, too, honors him so much that it sent to Iceland a great statue of him, which now stands before the school in Reyholt.

This presentation was to have been celebrated in 1941, on the seven hundredth anniversary of Snorri's death, but it was delayed on account of the war until August, 1947. Then the Crown Prince of Norway and his suite came to Iceland, and there was a tremendous celebration at Reyholt and the following week throughout all Iceland.

So the story of Snorri's own life is quite as interesting as some of the stories he told in his book *The Lives of the Norse Kings*.

## XV.     ICELANDERS AND AMERICANS

THERE is a wide street which runs out of the center of the city of Reykjavik, straight up a hill. On the top of this hill stands a great statue, which is visible from every direction. It shows a tall, powerful man in armor, with a flowing cloak thrown back from his shoulders. He is standing on a stone pedestal, which suggests the prow of a ship, looking towards the west, across the water towards America.

This statue represents Leif Eriksson, who discovered America in the year one thousand.

You remember reading that in 930 Iceland established the Althing at Thingvellir, and that it is the oldest Parliament in the world today. The United States, as a great and young democracy, wanted to honor this small and ancient democracy, and so, on the thousandth anniversary of the Althing, it gave this statue to Iceland.

Leif Eriksson's parents were Norwegians who had come to Iceland to settle there. His father was a chieftain named Eric the Red. His farm, which was called Erikstadir, was in Haukdalur, in the western part of Iceland. It was here that Leif was born, about 965.

The farm buildings have fallen down and grass grows over the place where they once stood. There is a river winding through the valley not far away, and emptying into a lake. We can imagine that when Leif was a little boy he liked to sail toy ships here.

We can also imagine him listening, during the long winter evenings, to the stories about Bjarni Herjolfson, who was a famous adventurer. Bjarni's parents, like Leif's, had been born in Norway and had come to Iceland to live, and Bjarni, like Leif, had been born there.

Bjarni was a great sailor and one time he thought he would like to sail to Greenland and find some of his relatives who were living there. He sailed and he sailed, but it was so foggy he could not see the sun or the moon or the stars, and without these to guide him, he got off his course. After twenty days the weather grew so warm that he knew he was far away from the cold shores of Greenland.

And then, to the great surprise of Bjarni and his companions, they saw a thickly wooded shore.

We think now that this was the shore of Newfoundland, but Bjarni had no idea where he was or what he was seeing, for at that time no one in Europe had ever heard of America. But Bjarni did not even go ashore. He had started out to find Greenland, so he turned around and went back, hunting for it. He did finally arrive there and looked up his relatives and made his visit.

When he went back home to Iceland, he told about the forested coast he had seen and Leif listened and wondered and determined that when he was a little older he would sail like Bjarni across the ocean. But he would not turn around without going ashore. He would make a thorough exploration.

He had to wait fourteen years before he was old enough to command his own ship.

Then he bought Bjarni's boat and chose thirty-five men to go with him. They sailed and they sailed and it was not until the forty-first day that they saw the dark line of a forested coast against the horizon. They came near enough to anchor and go ashore in a small boat.

They were astonished not to find any people there and they were almost as astonished to see how large the trees were, and how many kinds there were which they had never seen in Iceland.

They stayed on shore only a few hours, and then

rowed back to their ship and spent the night, for they did not know whether there might be some people hiding among the trees, who could attack them if they went to sleep on the shore.

The next day Leif and his men went ashore again and some of them explored in one direction and some in another. One of them discovered grapes growing, and afterwards they were able to make wine from them.

One thing they did recognize immediately, for they had often seen and eaten it in Iceland—and that was salmon. They speared a lot of these in a river and cooked them for dinner, and they must have tasted especially good to the explorers who had eaten nothing but ship's food for forty-two days.

The Icelanders spent a little more than a week on shore. They found several kinds of wild grain and some kernels of corn which they saved to carry back with them. They also took some dried grapes and various samples of wood to show the people at home what a rich country this was across the sea.

As they sailed away Leif said he would call the place Vinland (or Wineland) because grapes for wine making grew there. We do not know exactly where it was they came ashore. Some people think it was at what is now Maryland or Virginia. Other people feel sure it was at what is now Novia Scotia.

In any case, these were the first white men ever to step on the continent of North America. And that was why, when the people of the United States wanted to give a present to Iceland on her thousandth anniversary of the Althing, they decided it should represent Leif Eriksson.

At one time our Secretary of the Treasury began thinking that it would be a good thing if the United States could acquire Iceland. A few years later, after we had bought Alaska from Russia, our Secretary of State urged that we buy Iceland from Denmark.

Today the Icelanders like to laugh about this and say that, since Leif Eriksson discovered America, it would be more logical for Iceland to consider America as *her* colony.

After Leif's expedition, quite a few Icelanders came to the New World. Leif's younger brother, Thorvald, came, and he found Indians and fought with them, and he himself was killed by them. Another of Leif's brothers, Thorstein, made the journey, but, shortly after he had returned to Iceland, he died from the effects of the hard voyage. After Thorstein's death, his widow Gudrid, married a man named Thorfinn Karlsefni. Gudrid had gone to America with her first husband and always wanted to go back. Karlsefni had also wanted to see the new country, so they both crossed the ocean, and their baby was the first white child ever born on this conti-

GEORGE
GRAY
PHILADELPHIA

nent. This was at Chaleur Bay, in 1005. Karlsefni and Gudrid and their companions started a settlement, and we think this was somewhere on the New England coast. After three years, however, the settlement broke up and it was a long time before many Icelanders came to America again.

Einar Jonsson, the Icelandic sculptor, made a fine statue of Karlsefni which stands in Fairmount Park, in

Philadelphia. It shows him in a coat of mail, standing very straight indeed, with a round shield strapped behind his back and his two hands clasped on his long-handled battle-ax.

After our War Between the States the United States and Canada wanted more people to come and live in their countries. They offered free land, and sometimes a few farm animals, to people who would make good citizens.

At this time Iceland was very poor, and her people were unhappy under Danish rule. When they heard that there was a chance for them to own and cultivate land in the new world, they began to migrate in quite large numbers. Most of them settled in Manitoba and Saskatchewan, in Canada, but some moved to Minnesota and North Dakota, in the United States.

Of course, the winters are much colder and the summers much hotter in these places than they are in Iceland, and the newcomers suffered from both. However, they built houses and started their farms, and established Lutheran churches.

Those first settlers had to work hard, and even the small children had their duties. The men were kept busy chopping down trees and building houses, fishing and making hay. The hay was cut with a hand scythe and the women and young boys and girls all took a hand at spreading it out in the sun to dry.

The older children had to take the cows to the pastures in the morning and bring them back at night. It was not so difficult to drive them out, but finding them in the forest was no easy matter. The mosquitoes were thick, the sun was hot and often the searchers had to pick their way through marshes.

In places where there was not enough water, the wells might dry up in summer, and the children would have to go long distances to get a pailful to bring home. In the winter, they took pailfulls of snow and their mothers melted this on the kitchen stove.

There was plenty of fish, but those who did not live near a lake or a river had to travel for many hours to get this food. Some of the fish they saved for winter, by drying or smoking it, just as they had done in Iceland. In the evenings, the little girls and the little boys, too, helped their mothers, carding wool, spinning and knitting. Often the father would read aloud to the family as they worked. He might read the sagas or the Bible and everyone enjoyed the long evening.

The roads were so bad that people went to the store only a few times a year. Perhaps in the winter a pair of oxen would be hitched to a sleigh and plod slowly over the snow. It might take a week to make a trip we can do in less than a day by automobile. In summer, people traveled by boat, if possible. Coffee and tea and sugar were the chief things that had to be bought. Nearly everything else could be raised on the farm.

Of course, as the farms flourished, the work was not so hard and the roads were improved. Today some of those settlements of Icelanders, which were so small and poor, are up to date towns and the children of those children are college boys and girls.

While the first settlers soon learned to speak English, many of them liked to speak Icelandic in their homes. Today some of the children and grandchildren of those early settlers can speak Icelandic and are proud to observe certain Icelandic customs.

This does not mean that they are not good Americans, because they are. It means they still have an affection for their old homeland, and when they can, they like to go back there to visit.

You remember about the schools in Iceland—that every single child gets a good education. Wherever you find a group of Icelanders in the United States, you will find that their children are well educated and that frequently the older people not only read a great deal, but have their own newspapers and magazines.

A good many of them are farmers, and a good many more are doctors and lawyers and teachers. Some are in politics, but comparatively few in business. During the war, many Icelandic college boys and girls who could not go to Europe to finish their studies, came to the United States and Canada, so today in Reykjavik you can meet lots of Icelanders who have been in America.

After the war, some Icelandic girls married American soldiers and moved with them to the United States to live. Sometimes it has been the other way around, for Icelandic men who had been at school in the States have met and married American girls and taken them to Iceland.

Of all the Americans who have been to Iceland, there was one who admired the country so much that his name will never be forgotten in that connection. This was an American named Willard Fiske. In Chapter X, when you were learning about the birds and wild animals in Iceland, you read about the little island of Grimsey, which lies directly on the Arctic Circle.

There are only a few people who live there, but of course they have a church and a school and, of course, they are great readers. In the school, there is a small library which was given to them by Mr. Fiske. It seems that the people of Grimsey were very skillful chess players and Mr. Fiske was also fond of the game, so he gave them this library in recognition of the bond between them and him.

Mr. Fiske did more than this. He had collected many

Icelandic books, and he gave all of them to Cornell University. This is called the Willard Fiske Collection and it is one of the most complete Icelandic libraries in the world. There are some books in it which are not even in the National Library in Reykjavik.

While the Icelandic language is taught in some of the large American universities, and while the sagas are read and studied in our colleges, it was not until the Second World War that many Americans went to Iceland. During that time there were several thousands of our troops stationed there and some of them grew to know and like the Icelandic people and to admire the volcanic mountains and waterfalls and geysers of the country.

With planes constantly going back and forth between America and Iceland, and ships, too, it is no longer a hard, long journey, so every year more Icelanders and Americans come to know and like each other better.

*Arms of the President of Iceland*

## XVI.  IN AN ICELANDIC HOME

ICELANDERS are very fond of their homes and take
pleasure in buying paintings and sculptures for
them. We usually think that only wealthy people
can afford original oil paintings and pieces of statuary,
but in Iceland people who are not at all rich will save
money and deny themselves other things in order to
possess works of art.

They respect their painters and sculptors so much that

the government not only buys some of their artists' work, to make sure it is preserved, but it also gives some of the best of these artists a certain sum of money every year, so that they may continue to work without worrying about how they can support themselves and their families. It did this for Einar Jonsson, whose statue of Ingolf is the first one you see when you come into Reykjavik. The government also built Einar Jonsson a house, which is his for his lifetime. He designed it himself, and it is actually a good deal more than a house. There is a museum of his works on the first two floors, a studio above that, and on the top floor an apartment for the sculptor and his wife. The government plans to build another house next door to this one for the most popular painter, who is named Kjarvel.

Because so many people buy paintings, the artists in Iceland as a whole are better off than they are in the United States. And the average house is more decorated. Besides the paintings, sculpture and books to make the rooms attractive, they are cheerful and cozy because the women are such good housekeepers. They know how to cook excellent meals and they keep their houses neat and clean. They take especial care of the house plants which they arrange on their window sills. The outside of an apartment house may look bare and stern because there are so few shrubs and trees. But the vivid flowers or prettily trained vines seen through the windows brighten the front and back when seen from the street or from other windows.

Besides these potted plants, there are often cut flowers in a living room. People buy so many flowers that there are a great number of florists' shops in the cities. In fact, in the greenhouses which are heated by natural hot water there is more space given over to flowers than to vegetables.

In the cities, many people live in apartments, and in double or three or four family houses. But whether a child is brought up in an apartment or a house, he learns from an early age to love his home. When Christmas and other holidays come, they are usually celebrated at home, rather than in some public place.

Christmas begins at six o'clock on Christmas Eve.

There is a small tree—sometimes a real one and sometimes an artificial one, which has been brought from some other country. This usually stands on a table and the presents are gaily wrapped and put around it.

For dinner it is customary to have pea soup, smoked lamb and boiled potatoes and gravy. Sometimes there is ptarmigan—that bird which lives on the moors and whose plumage turns white in winter. There are lighted candles, and candy in colored paper bags, and maybe oranges or other fruit.

After everyone has opened his presents, the whole

family clasps hands and walks around the tree, singing Christmas hymns. This is called the first Christmas and is celebrated reverently. The next day is the second Christmas, when friends are invited and there are parties and all sorts of fun. In fact, Christmas celebrations sometimes go on until January the sixth. Christenings and birthdays give an opportunity for other parties.

All through the year there are holidays which are celebrated in different locations. For instance, in early August there is a three-day festival in the Westman Islands. You may remember some of the things you have read in this book about the Westman Islands: how the early Irishmen—or men from the West—fled thither; how the Algerian pirates once attacked them; and how they are the center for the codfishing. You remember, too, that it is here that men are let down by ropes to dangle over the steep, high cliffs and catch the seafowl and collect their eggs. This festival marks the end of the bird and egg season, and Icelanders come from all over the country to help the people in the Westman Islands celebrate the occasion.

Ever since earliest times, the Icelanders have been hospitable, both to their friends and to strangers. There is a story that once a wealthy landowner built his house in such a way it bridged the main road, so he could catch all travelers passing that way and invite them in to eat and drink. A big wedding party would last for a week, with every day filled with special events. Parties of a hundred or more invited guests were not uncommon. These tremendous celebrations were in those days when the early settlers were rich because they had brought so much silver with them from Norway. Both men and women wore arm rings of silver and heavy silver brooches held their cloaks together. They might wear homespun for every day, but their best clothes came from abroad, and were fashionably cut and of expensive materials. Some of the wealthiest women had silken underwear and silk and velvet dresses embroidered with gold. They had bracelets and rings and even golden diadems. The men—especially those who had traveled abroad in other countries—were proud of their closely-fitting long stockings and their coats which reached halfway down their legs—and might be of any bright color. Sometimes the men tied a silk band or ribbon around their foreheads, to keep their hair from blowing in their eyes. Men and women wore flowing capes and the richer in color and material, the better.

The houses in which such parties were celebrated might be handsomely decorated. To be sure, their walls were of rough stone and turf and their roofs were of turf, too, but sometimes there were embroidered tapestries on the walls, and the beams were carved and painted.

Sometimes the man of the house had brought carved columns from his home in Norway, and these were used in his high seat or throne. You remember that Ingolf brought such pillars with him and threw them overboard when he saw Iceland, and when he found where they had come ashore, he marked off his farm.

It was in such rooms that the skalds recited their verses and the storytellers repeated the sagas while everyone sat around and listened.

After those lavish and wealthy days came the centuries of volcanic eruptions, famines, diseases and Danish domination. Icelandic homes were hardly more than hovels, with dirt floors and grass roofs.

Today the homes are very similar to those in the United States.

In a city apartment or house, there will be a tiled kitchen, with an electric or gas stove and refrigerator. The bathroom will be tiled, also, and the other rooms will look quite a good deal like similar rooms in the States, except that there will probably be more pictures, pieces of sculpture and other ornaments in them.

In a house in the country, there may be the same comforts. If it is near a hot spring, there will be unlimited hot water, and if it is near a waterfall, there will be unlimited electricity. There will probably be more pictures, more books and more blossoming plants in the average room than in American rooms. Sometimes you may see a wire brush, which is used to clean and smooth a piece of wool, for the mother of the family, or one of the girls, may be carding (or combing) wool before spinning it into thread. You may see a loom for weaving or a pillow for lace making, with spools of gold or silver or white linen thread. Perhaps there is a piece of hand-weaving hanging on the wall and the rugs may be homemade, too.

From these things you will realize as soon as you step inside an Icelandic room that the people love their homes, and take pride in them and spend more time in them than many Americans do. The parties today may not be the magnificent affairs they were in the early days, but more like American parties. One thing about them is that, whatever kind of a party it is and at whatever the hour, there is sure to be coffee, for Icelanders are extremely fond of this drink and invariably make it properly. They have it for breakfast, in the middle of the morning, for luncheon, in the middle of the afternoon and before they go to bed at night. Sometimes, instead of putting a spoonful of sugar into the cup, they hold a lump of sugar between their teeth and drink the coffee through it. Usually they serve sweet bread or cakes or cookies with it, but best of all are the hot pancakes. These are like our griddle cakes or batter cakes, only very, very thin—almost as thin as paper. One such pancake fills a frying pan and when it is lifted out, it is spread with butter or sugar or jelly and rolled up. These pancakes are perfectly delicious and, although you may like them best when they are hot, they are very good cold, too. They are often served for breakfast as well.

Of course, the Icelanders do not stay at home all the time. The older people have their clubs and the younger people have their sports. They climb mountains and ski, and play all the games boys and girls play in America, and many of them are Boy or Girl Scouts. They go to church and they love moving pictures. Besides the moving picture houses, there is a Little Theatre in Reykjavik. It gives four or five plays every week during the season and they are always well attended. Besides the seats for three hundred people, the stage and dressing rooms, it has its restaurant where coffee is served during the intermission.

The splendid new National Theatre will, when it is finished, seat seven hundred people and will probably be just as popular as the Little Theatre has been.

In almost every town and village there are choral societies, whose members meet to sing together. Sometimes these small societies get together and form a larger group. There are more such societies in Iceland in comparison to its size than in any other country. One such group, called the Icelandic Singers, toured the United States and Canada in 1946. They gave fifty-six concerts in Icelandic and English, and were warmly welcomed and applauded wherever they went.

There are concerts, too, during the year, when foreign artists come to Reykjavik and these are always well attended. However, the Icelanders enjoy doing things themselves and not just listening to professional musicians or looking at pictures painted by well-known artists. They like to paint, and it is surprising how many men and women, boys and girls, who have other work or play to occupy them, find time to paint pictures in water colors and oils.

Many of the men and boys enjoy carving, and often in an Icelandic home you may see a carved chest or a table or the base of a lamp or a pair of bookends carved by someone in the family. If you should go to the National Museum, you would see objects carved by Icelanders hundreds and hundreds of years ago—bowls with and without covers, boxes, chairs, saddles, church furniture, etc., showing that this is an old art.

Quite a few of the girls know how to sew beautifully. They can make their own dresses and trim their own hats and, since they study the latest fashion magazines and go to see actresses in the latest movies, they know exactly what is the newest style, and are not content until they have achieved it.

It is possible that there is another reason why Icelandic

homes are cheerful. This is because no one feels that any-one else looks down on him. The family that lives in a three-room apartment is just as good as the family that lives in a fine, big house. Children are just as proud of a father who works on the docks as of a father who works in a bank. A boy who fishes or farms during the sum-mer to get money for his board and room at the Univer-sity during the winter is just as respected as the boy who goes abroad to study or travel during his vacation. A girl may be a waitress in a restaurant and her best friend may be the wife or daughter of a doctor.

Iceland is a true democracy. It does actually believe and practice that everyone is equal, and should have equal opportunity and justice. To be sure, everyone is not equally clever or equally kind or equally successful. But everyone has the same opportunity to be as clever, kind or successful as he can be. This means he may win as many friends or honors or make as much money as he is capable of winning or making.

Altogether Iceland is a happy country and the Ice-landers are a healthy and well educated people.

They admire the United States and are constantly learning from her citizens. The time has come for Ameri-cans—and people from other nations as well—to admire the Icelanders and learn from them, for their republic is the oldest one in the world, and has certain things to teach. We should not forget how bravely they held on during the Dark Ages of famine, disaster and misrule.

And we should not forget it was an Icelander who discovered America.

*Arms of Iceland as a Republic*

# INDEX

Alaska, 179
Algeria, 146-148
Althing, 17, 19, 65-68
America, discovery of, 175-179
animals, 35-38, 94-96
Arnason, Ingolf, 15-16, 191
Asbyrgi, 61-62
Auks, 96

basalt, 56
Bergthora, 114-118
birds, 96-105

caves, 61
Chaleur Bay, 180
Christian IV of Denmark, 146
Christianity, 71-75
Christianity, conversion to, 71-74
Christmas celebrations, 188-189
codfish, 77, 79, 82
colonists, 14-17, 73
cooperatives, 86-92
Copenhagen, 148
Cornell University, 184-185

Danish rule, 18, 68, 145, 181
Denmark, 17-18, 148
Dettifoss, 60
Drangey, 120

earthquakes, 54
education, 43-47
Eirikstadir, 176
emigration to U.S., 181-185
Eric the Red, 176
Eriksson, Leif, 175
Eriksson, Thorstein, 179
Eriksson, Thorvald, 179
exports, 78
Eystein, King, 161, 166-170

fairy tales, 124-143
falcon, 100-102
farming, 34-40
festivals, 67, 189-190
fishing, 76-84
Fiske, Willard, 105, 184-185
Floki, 14-15
flowers, 22, 25, 188
free land in U.S., 181
frozen fish, 79-82
fruits, 41, 57

# INDEX

Gilitrutt, 133-137
Gissur, 172-173
glaciers, 33-34, 53-54
Glaum, 120-124
Godafoss, 60, 72
Great Geysir, 58-59
Greenland, 176-177
Grettir the Strong, 118-124
Grimsey, 104, 184
Grimur Goatbeard, 65
Gruman boats, 84
Gudmundur Einarsson, 105
Gudridur Simonardsdottir,
    147-150
Gullfoss, 60
Gunnar, 114-118
Gyda, 159-160
gymnastics, 47-48

Hallgerda, 115-118
Hallgrimur Petursson, 148-154
Harald Gormson, King, 160-
    161
Haukdalur, 176
Hegranes, 122
Hekla, 52-53
Helga and the Elves, 137-141
Herjolfson, Bjarni, 176-177
herring, 77-78, 82, 84-85
Hlini, 127-133
holidays, 188-189
home life, 187-195
hot springs, 8-11, 57-59

Hurdy-Gurdy, 57
Hveragerdi, 57

Icelandic singers, 193-194
Illugi, 120-124
imports, 26-28
Ingolf, 15-16, 191
Ireland, 73

Jonsson, Einar, 180, 187

Karlsefni, Thorfinn, 179-181
Keflavik, 4-6
Kjarvel, 187

Lawman, 66-67
laws, 66-68
legends, 62, 71
Lives of Norse Kings, 156
Lutheranism, 74-75

Maiden's Seat, 67
Manitoba, 181
Maryland, 178
Minnesota, 2, 181
Mohammedan religion, 147-
    150
monks, 14, 73-74
Myvatn, Lake, 54-55

National Library, 185
National Museum, 194
national park, 70

# INDEX

National Theatre, 193
Nevjolvson, Toraren, 171-172
Newfoundland, 177
Njals Saga, 114
Norse language, 108-109
North Dakota, 181
Norway, 17
Nova Scotia, 178

Order of the Icelandic Falcon,
    102-103
Oxara, 65

Papey, 73
Passion Hymns, 152
Petursson, Hallgrimur, 148-
    154
Philadelphia, 180-181
pirates, 19, 144-147
plagues, 54
playgrounds, 48
postage stamps, 69, 85

religion, 71-75
republic declared, 68-69
Reyholt, 155-156
Reykjavik, 3, 11-12, 21-30, 32,
    57

sagas, 112-124
Saskatchewan, 181

schools, 43-47
Siglufordur, 79, 84-85
Signy, 127-133
Sigurd, King, 166-170
Simonardsdottir, Gudridur,
    147-150
Skalds, 110-112
Skalholt, 141
slaves, 74
sloyd, 43-44
Snorri, 8,156-173
Sourby, 151
sports, 47-50
St. Olav (King Olav), 162-165
Sturlason, Snorri, 8, 156-173
sulphur, 55
Surtshellir, 61

Things, 65
Thingvellir, 64, 70-71
travel, 22, 31-33
Trygvason,Olav, 157-160
turf huts, 39-40

vegetables, 9, 57
Vestfjords, 145
Vikings, 13-14, 16, 64, 73
Vinland, 178
Virginia, 178
volcanoes, 5-6, 18-19, 51-55

Westman Islands, 73, 146, 189